IN CHAINS TO
LOUISIANA

Black Autobiographies

IN CHAINS TO LOUISIANA

SOLOMON NORTHUP'S STORY
adapted by MICHAEL KNIGHT

A Richard W. Baron Book

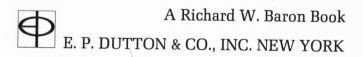

E. P. DUTTON & CO., INC. NEW YORK

Solomon Northup's story was first published in 1853 as *Twelve Years a Slave. Narrative of Solomon Northup, a Citizen of New-York, Kidnapped in Washington City in 1841, and Rescued in 1853, from a Cotton Plantation near the Red River, in Louisiana.*

Published simultaneously in Canada by Clarke, Irwin & Company Limited, Toronto and Vancouver

SBN: 0-525-32540-9
Library of Congress Catalog Card Number: 73-108967
Printed in the U.S.A.
First Edition

Black Autobiographies is a series designed to bring back to life in modern language a rich heritage of first-person stories obscured too long by dust and the formal English prose of the eighteenth and nineteenth centuries. The original accounts were written by black men and women, most of them ignored by history. They tell of slavery, escape, kidnapping, bravery, suffering, triumph, war, and everyday life in times long gone.

CONTENTS

IN CHAINS TO LOUISIANA

CHAPTER 1

Kidnapped

May, 1853

I WAS BORN a free black man, unlike the millions of black men in the southern states who are slaves, the property of other men. But one day I woke up from a drugged sleep to find myself in chains, a slave without my freedom. And, it seemed, without any hope of ever being free again.

But then, let me start my story at the very beginning.

My father, Mintus Northup, was born a slave owned by the Northup family of Rhode Island. We took our name from that family, and they gave us our freedom. My father's master put it in his will that when he died, my father should be a free man. All this must have happened about fifty years ago, around the year 1800. Before that, as far as I can find out, my father's family had always been slaves in Rhode Island. But his master left Rhode Island and came to the state of New York, where I was born in July, 1808, near the small town of Minerva, about 200 miles north of New York City in the Adirondack Mountains. I was named Solomon.

My father, my mother, my brother, Joseph, and I moved from farm to farm over the years, until November, 1829, when my father died. Joseph lives near Oswego, in upstate New York. My mother died during the years I was a slave in the sickly swamps and forests of Louisiana.

My father was a man known for his honesty and hard work. He enjoyed the peaceful life of farming. He never had to look for the menial work that seems reserved especially for black men, and he was able to give us an education better than most black children. He even gathered enough property—worth $100—to entitle him to the right to vote, under the laws of that time. It was an unusual thing for a black man.

On Christmas Day that year, 1829, I married Anne Hampton, who lived nearby in Sandy Hill at the Eagle Tavern, where she was becoming famous as a good cook. She is unable to tell the exact history of her family, but the blood of three races is in her veins. I don't know if she is more black, red, or white, but the combination is very pretty.

I was just past my twenty-first birthday, without the help and advice of my father, and with a wife to support now. I decided to begin a life of honest hard work like my father's. I dreamed of someday having a house of my own and a few acres to farm.

As soon as possible after the wedding, Anne and I moved into an old yellow house in nearby Fort Edward, a house that had been occupied by the British General "Gentleman Johnny" Burgoyne in 1777 in the War for Independence. During the winter I worked on repairing the Champlain Canal, which runs between the towns of Hudson Falls and Whitehall. It connects the Hudson River with Lake Champlain, making it possible for boats to travel from New York City as far as Montreal, in Canada.

By the time the canal opened in the spring of 1830, after the ice melted, I had saved enough money to buy a pair of horses and hire a few helpers. I went into the business of floating rafts of lumber from Lake Champlain to the city of Troy. I became good at rafting, a very difficult job, and once went as far north as Montreal and other cities in the area.

By the next spring, Anne and I decided to rent a farm in the neighborhood. So I arranged to take part of a farm in Kingsbury that my father had once worked. With one cow, a pig, and a pair of oxen, we made our new home. That year I planted twenty-five acres of corn and sowed a large field of oats. Those were good years, with Anne working in the house, while I worked in the field.

In the winters, I was often asked to play the violin; whenever the young people gathered to dance, I was almost always there. Anne began earning good wages as a cook in town on holidays and during those weeks when the court of law was in session there. Between cooking, fiddling, and farming, we were well off and had a happy and prosperous life. It would have been best for us if we had stayed on that farm. But in 1834, we moved to Saratoga Springs. It was a resort full of rich people who came for the mineral water of the famous spring to drink and to bathe in. They came also to bet on the horse races, and sometimes to win, sometimes to lose money at the gambling casino just outside of town. The richest and most fashionable people stayed at the United States Hotel, where Anne and I worked during the summer season. During the winter I relied on my violin and helped build the railroad between Troy and Saratoga.

While living at the hotel, I often met with slaves up from the South with their masters. They were always well-dressed and well taken care of, leading an easy life without any worry about making a living. We often talked about slavery and almost always I found that they secretly wanted to escape. But their fear of punishment was always enough to stop them from trying.

Having been a free man all my life, I could not understand how anyone could live as a slave. I still cannot understand how laws can make slavery legal, or why religions do not object to it. Never once, I'm proud to say, did I fail to tell any slave who asked me: watch for your chance and then run for your freedom.

We continued to live in Saratoga for the next seven years, but we had not done as well as we hoped. Although we were not poor, we were not better off than before. By this time also we were the parents of three children—Elizabeth, the oldest, was ten, Margaret was two years younger, and little Alonzo was just five. When I wasn't working, I was out walking with them through the streets of Saratoga, proud as any father, black or white, could be.

One morning in late March, 1841, I was wandering around the town with nothing else to do and wondering where to find work. Anne was away for the week in Sandy Hill, cooking at the tavern. On the corner of Congress Street and Broadway I was introduced to two gentlemen who were called Merrill Brown and Abraham Hamilton—although I now doubt that those were their real names. They asked me about my violin playing, and offered to hire me for a short time. They worked, they said, with a circus in Washington, D.C., and were going south to rejoin it. They offered me a dollar a day and three dollars for each night I played at one of their shows, if I would go with them. I accepted the offer at once, because the pay was good and because I liked the idea of traveling and the chance to see the city of Washington.

Merrill Brown was a man about forty years old, with a shrewd and intelligent face. He wore a black coat and a black hat, and said that he came from Rochester or Syracuse. Abraham Hamilton was young, under twenty-five, with a fair complexion and light eyes, and was elegantly dressed. I trusted them completely. Their conversation with me and their attitude toward me was kind and generous. I was convinced they were my friends.

So, thinking that I would be gone for only a few days, I took a change of clothes and my violin and left without bothering to write to Anne, since I thought I would return before she would. We left Saratoga that morning in a covered carriage drawn by a pair of horses. As our horses took us stylishly along the road to Albany under bright skies, I felt as happy, I think, as I have ever been in my life.

We reached the state capital before dark, and stopped at a hotel. That night I had my first and last chance to watch them perform. Hamilton stood at the door, collecting tickets. I played my violin. And Brown juggled balls, danced on a rope, fried pancakes in a hat, made invisible pigs squeal, and did other tricks of that kind. The audience was very small, and the earnings, according to Hamilton, were not much more than "a beggarly account of empty boxes."

We started out again early the next morning. We hurried ahead without stopping to perform, and toward nightfall we reached New York City, where we stayed at a hotel on the city's West Side. The next day, Brown and Hamilton suggested that, since we were about to enter a state where slavery was legal, it would be wise to get "free papers" for me in New York. The idea seemed good, although I would never have thought of it myself, and so we went downtown to the Customs House, near the ferryboats to Staten Island. There I swore that I was a free man, and the papers were made out. After paying a clerk two dollars, I received my papers, stamped and sealed, and we started back to the hotel. At the time I thought getting the papers hardly worth the trouble. The clerk made a record of it all in a large book, which is probably still there in the Customs House for all to see.

With the free papers in my pocket, I crossed the ferry to Jersey City with my new friends, and we took the road to Philadelphia. All the way their eagerness to rejoin the circus grew and grew. We arrived in Washington the evening before the funeral of General William Henry Harrison, the Indian fighter, hero of the battle of Tippecanoe, and ninth President of the United States. He had caught pneumonia just a month after becoming President, and died.

The funeral the next day was a great pageant. The air was filled with the sounds of roaring cannons and tolling bells. Many houses were shrouded in black crepe bunting, and the streets were full of people. In the afternoon, the funeral procession came by, carriage after carriage moving to the sound of mournful music, bearing the body of Harrison to the grave.

I spent the day with Hamilton and Brown, the only people I knew in Washington. I remember how the window glass broke and rattled to the ground after each cannon fired at the burial ground. We visited the Capitol later and then the White House, but I never did see the circus, and, in the excitement of the day, never thought of it. Later we stopped at a saloon, and, after serving themselves, my two friends poured me a drink or two. I did not become drunk. But toward evening, pains began in my head, and I felt dull and heavy. I felt hot all over and thirsty, and went to bed, unable to eat anything.

I was up all night getting water, until I was too weak to get up anymore. Sometime during the night I remember three people entering my room and taking me to what they said was a doctor's house. I remember going with them. And then all I can remember is that when I woke—was it the next morning or days later?—I was in a completely dark room, with my head still painful. And I was in chains.

CHAPTER 2

The Slave Pen

I FELT VERY faint and weak. I was sitting on a low bench, made of rough boards, and I was handcuffed. One end of a heavy pair of chains was fastened to my ankles, and the other end to a large iron ring in the floor. I listened hard for a long while, but I could hear nothing but the clinking of my chains. I felt in my pockets and found that not only was my money gone, but also my free papers. For the first time, I understood what was happening. The more I thought about it, the surer I became that I had been kidnapped and sold.

About three hours later, I heard footsteps overhead, and I thought that I must be in some sort of underground dungeon. The footsteps continued for a while, and then I heard a key rattle in the lock. A strong door swung back, light flooded the room, and two men entered and stood in front of me.

One was a large, powerful man, forty years old,

with dark hair turning gray. His face showed nothing but cunning and cruelty. Later I learned that he was James H. Birch, a well-known slave dealer in Washington.

With him was his assistant, Ebenezer Radburn.

I could now see the room for the first time. It was about twelve feet square with solid stone walls. The door led through a small passage up a flight of stairs to a yard surrounded by a wall ten or twelve feet high. I was to discover that the building to which the yard was attached was two stories high, and, from the outside, it looked like any private house. A stranger looking at it would never have guessed what it was used for. Looking down on the house, from a height, was the Capitol. The voices of patriotic representatives boasting of freedom and equality were almost close enough to mix with the rattling of poor slaves' chains—a slave pen in the shadow of the Capitol!

"Well, my boy, how do you feel now?" Birch asked as he entered the room and opened the shutter on a small window.

"I'm sick," I answered. "What am I doing here?"

"You are my slave—I bought you, and I'm sending you to New Orleans in a few days," he said, pleasantly enough.

"I'm a free man from New York. My name is Solomon Northup," I said loudly and boldly. I complained bitterly about my treatment. And I threatened that once I was free again, they would pay for it.

"A free man? You?—you're my slave, up from Georgia," he answered, not pleasant at all now. Again and again, I shouted that I was free. I insisted that Birch take the chains off at once. He tried to hush me, as if he were afraid that someone would hear.

Finally, seeing that he could not keep me quiet, he flew into a rage, called me a black liar, a runaway from Georgia, and every other thing he could think of.

Radburn watched the two of us. His job was to watch over this human stable, receiving slaves, feeding and whipping them. Birch turned to him and ordered the paddle and the cat-o'-nine-tails.

The paddle, as it is called in slave-beating language, is made of hard wood eighteen or twenty inches long and is shaped like an oar. The cat was a large rope made of many loose strands with a knot tied at the end of each.

They grabbed me and tore my clothing off. My feet were already chained to the floor, and they bent me over the bench, face down. Radburn stepped on the chain between my hands, and I was pinned down. Birch started to beat me with the paddle, and when he got tired, he stopped and asked me if I still thought I was free. I said I was.

Then he hit me harder and harder. He got tired again, and again he asked me the same question. I gave him the same answer.

Finally the paddle broke. He could not force me to say that I was a slave. He got angrier and angrier then and picked up the cat-o'-nine-tails. This hurt a lot more than the paddle. I struggled and prayed, but all I got were more lashes.

At last I was quiet and would not answer at all.

In fact I almost could not talk anymore. But Birch kept beating me. A man with any human pity would not have beaten a dog so hard. Finally, Radburn said that there was no point in beating me anymore. "He is sore enough," he told Birch.

Birch stopped, grabbed me by the throat, shook his fist in my face, and hissed through clenched teeth: "If you ever dare say again that you are free, or that you were free—this beating will be nothing compared to what you'll get. Do as I say, or I'll kill you. I'd rather see you dead than free!"

The chains were taken off my hands, the door quickly shut behind them, and I was left alone again in the darkness.

An hour or two later, the key rattled in the door again. Now I was afraid of any human face, especially a white one. Radburn entered, carrying a tin plate with a piece of shriveled fried pork, a slice of bread, and a cup of water.

"How do you feel?" he asked me. "You had a pretty bad beating. You better not say anything again about freedom," he added. "Take my advice: the less you say about it, the better it will be for you."

I wasn't sure if he was trying to be kind, or whether Birch was just trying another way to keep me quiet. Radburn unlocked my chains, opened the shutter on the little window, and left.

By this time I was stiff and sore, and my body was covered with blisters. At night, I lay down on the damp floor without any pillow or cover. Twice a day Radburn came in with his pork, bread, and water.

My wounds would not let me stay in one position long, and I spent most of my time moving from one position to another.

But still my spirit was not broken. I still thought of escaping. It was impossible, I thought, that anyone would keep me as a slave if he knew the truth. I thought that if Birch found out that I was not a runaway from Georgia, he would let me go. Surely Brown and Hamilton would find me soon and get me out.

After a few days, the door was opened, and I was allowed to go into the yard. There were three slaves there. One of them was a boy of about ten. The others were young men of about twenty and twenty-five.

The oldest was named Clemens Ray. He had lived in Washington, and driven a hack, and worked in a stable for a long time. He was very bright and understood how bad a spot we were in. He was full of grief about going south. Birch had bought him a few days before, and was keeping him here until he was ready to send him to the New Orleans slave market. He told me that we were in Williams's Slave Pen.

I told him my story.

"You better be quiet about it," he said. "Birch will only whip you more if he hears you."

The next oldest was John Williams, from Virginia. Birch took him instead of payment for a debt, and Williams constantly hoped that his old master would pay the debt and take him back.

The boy was called Randall. Most of the time he played around the yard, but sometimes he would cry, calling for his mother and wondering when she would come for him. He was too young to realize what was happening, and, when he wasn't thinking of his mother, he was happy playing.

At night I was locked in my cell, while the others slept in a loft. We were all given horse blankets, the only bedding of any sort I was to have for the next twelve years. Ray and Williams asked me many questions about New York State, how black people were treated there, how they could have homes and families of their own. Ray, especially, wished he were free. When we talked, we made sure that we could not be heard by Birch or Radburn.

I stayed at Williams's Slave Pen about two weeks. The night before we left, Randall's mother and little sister were brought in, crying. They hugged Randall to them. Emily, the girl, was about seven or eight years old with a light skin and a beautiful face. Her hair fell in curls around her neck, and she was dressed in expensive clothing. The woman was dressed in silk, with rings on her fingers and golden earrings. The way she carried herself and spoke showed that she had at some time been something more than a slave. She seemed amazed at finding herself in such a place.

Complaining loudly, she was herded, with her children and myself, into the cell, and we were locked up for the night. Her name was Eliza, and this was the story she told:

She was the slave of Elisha Berry, a rich man who lived near Washington. She was born on his plantation. Years ago, Berry quarreled with his wife and left her. He set up housekeeping on the plantation with Eliza. He promised her that she and any children they had would have their freedom if she lived with him as a wife. So she lived there nine years, with servants to work for her and every comfort and luxury. Emily and Randall were Berry's children.

Finally, Mrs. Berry's daughter married a man named Jacob Brooks. And, after a while, for some reason not clear to me, Mr. Berry lost all his property. Part of it, including Eliza and her children, went to Brooks. During the nine years that Eliza had lived with Berry, Mrs. Berry and her daughter got to hate her deeply.

The day she was led into the pen, Brooks had brought her from the plantation to the city, saying that the time had come for her free papers to be made out. Overjoyed, she dressed herself and Emily in their best clothes and accompanied him. But the papers were not free papers. They were bills of sale, made out to Birch the slave trader.

CHAPTER 3

Going to New Orleans

ABOUT MIDNIGHT the next day, the cell door opened, and Birch and Radburn entered. They woke us up with curses and kicks and hustled us out of the cell. We were all handcuffed, and Clem Ray and I were handcuffed together. John Williams was not with us anymore. He was still a slave, but he was a happy man: his master had bought him back from Birch.

It was a dark and quiet night. I could see the lights over toward Pennsylvania Avenue, where the White House is, but there was no one on the streets. If it weren't for the handcuffs, I would have tried to run away as they marched us down the empty streets to the Potomac River.

We reached a steamboat after a while, and were quickly hustled down into the hold, with the boxes and barrels of freight. The engine steamed up, the paddle wheel turned, and we set off down the river. The ship's bell tolled as we passed the tomb of

George Washington, and Birch bowed his head.

None of us slept that night except little Randall and Emily. Both Clem and Eliza cried all night. I tried to keep up my spirits, spending the night thinking of ways to escape. I was set to take the first chance that came along. By now, I had made up my mind not to say anything more about being born free—it would only make escape harder.

In the morning, the ship docked at a small town, and we changed to a stagecoach. Birch laughed and played with the children, and once he even bought them a piece of gingerbread. At Fredericksburg, we transfered to a train. Before dark, we were at Richmond, capital of the slave state of Virginia. We were driven through the streets to a slave pen, owned by a man named Goodin.

Goodin met us at the door. He was short and fat, with a plump, dark face. He and Birch seemed to be old friends. They shook hands for a long time. Then Goodin turned to me, grabbing me by the arm and turning me around. He looked at me sharply, like someone who thinks of himself as a good judge of property. He seemed to be figuring out how much I was worth.

"Well, boy, where did you come from?" he asked.

For a moment I forgot what I had decided. "From New York," I said.

"New York, hell! What have you been doing up there?" He looked astonished.

Birch had an angry, murderous look in his eyes that was not hard to understand.

I answered as quickly as I could, "Oh, I have been only up there for a while."

Goodin seemed satisfied, and turned to Clem, and then to Eliza and the children. "All together a fair lot—a devilish good lot," he announced after a while.

There were about thirty slaves in the pen when we were pushed into it. They were all cleanly dressed, the men with hats, and the women with handkerchiefs tied around their heads.

Some time later, Birch came down to the yard, took off my handcuffs, and led me into one of the small houses nearby.

"You told that man you came from New York," he said.

"I told him I had been up as far as New York," I corrected. "I didn't tell him I was a free man. I meant no harm at all, Master Birch."

He looked at me for a moment as if he were going to kill me, then turned around and left. In a few moments he returned. "If I ever hear you say a word about New York, or about your freedom, I will be the death of you—I will kill you; you may rely on that."

He understood better than I did how dangerous it was to sell a free man into slavery. My life would not have meant a thing to him if he felt that his crime might be discovered by the law. Clearly, he meant what he said.

After dinner, I was handcuffed to a large man named Robert. Like myself, he had been born free. He had a wife and two children in Cincinnati. Rob-

ert said that he came south with two men who had
offered to hire him. Without free papers, he had been
grabbed at Fredericksburg and placed in a cell.
There he was beaten until he had learned, as I had,
how important it was to keep quiet. He had been in
Goodin's pen about two weeks. We became friends.

Robert, Clem, Eliza and the children, and I slept
in one of the small houses in the yard that night.
There were four others with us, including a man
named David and his wife, Caroline. They were worried about being sent south to the cane and cotton
fields, but they worried even more about being separated. There was also Mary, a tall girl who had been
born a slave and was uneducated. She was afraid of
nothing but the whip, and knew nothing else. And
there was also Lethe, whose husband had been sold
from her. She no longer knew or cared where she was.
A change of masters, she felt, could hardly be for the
worse.

In the morning, Clem Ray was told that he was
going back to Washington for some reason. He was
overjoyed. Shaking hands, we parted, and I have not
seen him since. But, much to my surprise, I later
learned that he had escaped and made his way up to
Canada. He even spent a night in my brother-in-
law's house in Saratoga.

In the afternoon, we were handcuffed and driven
through the streets to the *Orleans*, a sailing ship full
of tobacco.

Birch put us on the ship and left for Washington.
That was the last I saw of him for a long time. James

H. Birch was a slave trader, buying men, women, and children at low prices and selling them for a profit. He was a merchant in human flesh, a profession looked down on even in the South.

The ship set sail, and we arrived at Norfolk, Virginia, the next day. Four more slaves came on board there. Frederick was a boy of eighteen, and Harry was a few years older. There was also Maria, a pretty girl, but ignorant and vain. The idea of going to New Orleans seemed like a lot of fun to her. Surely, she told us, some wealthy man with good taste would buy her right away.

The most noticeable of the four was a man named Arthur, who struggled with his keepers constantly, demanding to be released. His face was swollen and covered with wounds and bruises. One side of it was completely raw. He was forced down the hatchway and into the hold. Later, he told me his story:

He had lived in Norfolk a long time as a free man, and he had a family there. He was a mason by trade, and, coming home late after a long day of laying bricks, he was attacked, bound, and gagged. A few days later, he found himself on the ship with us.

The captain chose Robert as his waiter for the trip, and I was appointed to oversee the cooking and the sharing out of food and water.

We ate twice a day—always boiled bacon and hoe-cakes made of cornmeal, sweetened with molasses and scorched in a kettle.

People who have never been chained and beaten, carried away from home and family, or treated like an animal, might find it hard to forgive what I'll tell next. But what would they do in our position?

Arthur and I were in the bow of the ship one evening, talking about the future that stretched before us. Arthur said, and I agreed, that death was far better. For a while, we talked about our wives, children, our past lives, and the possibility of escape. And then, we talked about killing the crew, taking over the ship, and heading for New York. We both liked the idea. We tried to figure out our chances against the crew. Who could be relied on and who could not? When could we strike and how?

While the others slept, Arthur and I worked out our plans. We told Robert cautiously, and he was with us right away. There was not another slave we dared trust. They are brought up in fear and ignorance, and they cringe if a white man even frowns at them. It was not safe to let people like that in on our plans. The three of us decided to do it all ourselves.

Each night we were forced down into the hold and locked in, so how to reach the deck was our first problem. We decided to see what would happen if we hid under the small boat on the deck when the rest were sent below decks, to see if we would be missed. I was the one who would test the idea, and the next night I slipped away from the others and hid under the boat. In the morning I rejoined the others as they were let out. No one had noticed a thing.

Robert, who was allowed into the captain's cabin as the ship's waiter, told us that there were always two pistols and a sword on the table there. The cook slept in the galley, and the sailors slept in hammocks in the forecastle.

Finally, our plans were complete. We would hide under the boat at night, slip into the captain's cabin, take the pistols and the sword, and kill him as quickly as possible. We left everything else to be decided on the spot. If the attack was so sudden that there was no resistance, we would keep the hatch locked until later. If there was trouble, we would let the slaves out and hope to save ourselves in the confusion and panic.

We were all ready, when something we could not have expected happened. Robert came down with the terrible smallpox. He died four days before we reached New Orleans. One of the sailors sewed him up in a blanket, weighed down with stones, and he was dumped over the side.

We were all afraid of smallpox, which can spread quickly in so small a space as we had. Our plans were forgotten.

An evening or two after Robert's funeral, I was leaning on the hatchway near the forecastle, full of gloomy thoughts. A sailor with a kind voice asked me why I was so downhearted. I answered that I was a free man and had been kidnapped.

"That's enough to make anyone downhearted," he said. And he asked more questions until he had my whole story. He promised to help, even if, as he put it in sailor talk, it would "split my timbers."

I asked him to get me a pen and paper and ink and a small piece of candle. The next night I hid under the boat and wrote a letter to Henry B. Northup of Sandy Hill—whose people had freed my father a long time ago. I told him where I was and what had happened. I asked him to rescue me.

My friend's name was John Manning. He was an Englishman, about twenty-four years old, and he had lived in Boston for a while.

Nothing much happened until we docked in New Orleans. As soon as the ship was tied to the levee, Manning jumped to shore and hurried toward the city. As he left, he looked back at me. When he returned, he gave me a wink, as if to say that the letter had been mailed and everything was all right.

I later found out that the letter reached Sandy Hill. Mr. Northup took it to Albany and gave it to Governor William Seward. But since it didn't say where I was going after New Orleans, they decided to wait for further word.

Just after Manning left the ship, two men came up and called for Arthur. He was almost crazy with happiness, and he could hardly keep from jumping over the side to them. When they came aboard, he hugged them for a long time. They were friends from Norfolk, who had come to rescue him. They told him that his kidnappers were in jail. The two men left soon afterward with Arthur.

But in all the crowd on the levee, there was no one to meet me. No one, no familiar face, no familiar voice. Soon Arthur would rejoin his family. I wondered if I would ever see mine again.

After a while, traders and owners came aboard.

One, named Theophilus Freeman, called for Birch's gang. Reading his paper, he called "Platt," but no one came forward. He called again and again, but there was no reply. Then Lethe was called, then Eliza, and then the rest.

"Captain, where's Platt?" he demanded.

The captain didn't know what to say. No one on board was called Platt.

"Who shipped that nigger?" he asked, pointing at me.

"Birch," the captain answered.

"Your name is Platt—you answer my description. Why don't you come forward?" he asked angrily.

"That's not my name. I've never been called Platt, but I have no objection to it."

"Well, I'll learn you your name so you won't forget it," he finished.

Platt was the name Birch gave me on the shipping papers, and it was the name I was to have for a long time.

CHAPTER 4

Smallpox and Sale

THEOPHILUS FREEMAN, keeper of the slave pen in New Orleans, was out among his animals early in the morning. With an occasional kick at the older men and women and sharp cracks of the whip at the younger ones, he soon had us awake and moving around. Freeman was getting his property ready for sale, and he intended to do a brisk business.

We were told to wash, and those of us with beards had to shave them off. We were each given a new suit of cheap cotton clothes and led into a large room in the front of the building. The men had to line up on one side of the room and the women on the other. The tallest stood at one end of each line, the shortest at the other. Freeman warned us to remember to be bright and lively and taught us to "look smart."

In the afternoon, we were paraded around again and forced to dance. Bob, a slave who had worked with Freeman for some time, played the violin for the dancing. I was standing near him, and boldly asked if he could play a Virginia reel. He said that he couldn't and handed me his violin. Freeman was very pleased to see what a talented slave he had, and he made me play for a long while.

The next day, the customers came to examine Freeman's "new lot." They made us hold up our heads, walk briskly back and forth. They felt our hands and arms and bodies, turned us around, asked us what we could do, and made us open our mouths and show our teeth the way a jockey examines a horse. Sometimes a man or woman would be taken to a small house in the back and stripped for a closer look. If a slave had scars on his back, he was taken for a troublemaker, and that knocked down his price.

One old gentleman wanted a coachman, and he seemed interested in buying me. I found out that he lived in New Orleans, and I hoped that he would buy me. From New Orleans, I thought, I might be able to escape on some ship bound for the North. But Freeman wanted $1,500 for me, and the old gentleman insisted that that was too much. Freeman argued that I was sound, healthy, and intelligent and could play the violin.

"There's nothing extraordinary about the nigger," the old man argued. He left, saying that he might return another day. I was very disappointed.

Later that day, David and Caroline were bought as a pair by a planter from Natchez, Mississippi. They were very happy not to be separated. Lethe was bought by a planter from Baton Rouge, Louisiana, and the same man also bought little Randall.

The boy had to jump and run and do a lot of other things to show that he was strong and healthy. Eliza cried while this was going on, and she pleaded with the planter not to buy Randall, unless he also bought her and Emily. The man answered that he could not afford them, and then Eliza burst out with shouts of grief.

Freeman turned to her, raised his whip, and ordered her to be quiet. "Stop snivelling, or you'll get a hundred lashes," he snarled. Eliza tried to wipe away her tears, but she loved her children and wanted to be with them. She kept on begging and pleading, but it was no use. The man could not afford it. The bargain was made, and Randall had to go. Eliza ran to him, kissed him again and again, and told him to remember her. Freeman swore and cursed the whole time.

"Don't cry, Mama," Randall shouted as he was led out the door. "I'll be a good boy. Don't cry, Mama."

I would have cried myself, if I had dared.

That night, nearly all of us who had come on the ship got sick, complaining of terrible pains in the head and back. In the morning, a doctor came, but he couldn't tell what the matter was. While he examined me, I told him that I thought it might be smallpox, since Robert had died of it at sea. "It might be so, indeed," he agreed, and sent for Dr. Carr, the head of the hospital.

After a while, Dr. Carr came and said that we all did have the smallpox, which frightened everyone.

Eliza, Harry, Emily, and I were taken to the hospital, and I became very sick. For three days I was blind, and the doctor said that Platt was in very bad shape, but that he might survive. I expected to die, and was almost happy at the thought.

There were a lot of people in the hospital. In the rear of the building, coffins were made. And when someone died, the bell was rung as a signal to the undertaker to come and take the body away. The bell tolled many times, but the crisis passed, and I began to recover.

After two weeks, Harry and I were brought back to the pen. Both of us had the permanent marks of smallpox on our faces. Eliza and Emily were brought back the next day. Neither had been seriously ill. We were paraded in front of the customers again that day, and I hoped that the old gentleman would return, but he didn't.

After a few days, a planter named William Ford came to buy slaves. He was from Louisiana's bayou section, where the land is all cut up by streams from the Mississippi River on their way down to the Gulf of Mexico. His plantation was on Bayou Boeuf in Avoyelles Parish, near the Red River. After inspecting us all, he offered Freeman $1,000 for me, $900 for Harry, and $700 for Eliza. I can't say whether the smallpox lowered our price. But Freeman thought about it for a while and then accepted.

As soon as Eliza heard it, she was crying in agony again. She left her place in the line and rushed down to where Emily was standing and hugged her. Freeman ordered her back, but she ignored him. He grabbed her arm and pulled her away, but she broke away and hugged the child again. Then he hit her, and she almost fell.

"Mercy, master, mercy," she cried, getting down on her knees in front of Ford. "Please, master, buy my Emily. I can never work any if she is taken from me. I will die."

She pleaded for a long while, telling Ford how Randall had been taken from her.

Finally, Ford went up to Freeman and asked, "How much do you want for the little girl?"

"What is her *price? Buy* her?" Freeman answered with a sneer. "She's not for sale."

Ford said that he didn't need anyone so young, but since the mother was so fond of her, he would pay a reasonable price. "I said she's not for sale. In a few years a lot of men will pay plenty for her," he answered.

That only made Eliza worse. "I will not go without her. They can't take me from her," she shrieked.

Meanwhile, Harry and I were coming back from the yard, where we had gone to get our blankets. We waited for a while, and then Freeman tore Emily away.

"Don't leave me, Mama—don't leave me," Emily screamed, as her mother was pulled away. "Come back, Mama." But her crying did her no good.

Out the door and into the street we were hurried. We could hear her voice for blocks, until finally it died away in the distance.

CHAPTER 5

At Ford's Plantation

WILLIAM FORD had his plantation in the Great Pine Woods of Avoyelles Parish, on Bayou Boeuf, a small stream that flows into the Red River in the heart of Louisiana. He is a Baptist preacher, and on both sides of the bayou he is well liked and respected. To many people, the idea that a man of God could own slaves seems strange and impossible, and from what I've said of Birch and Freeman, many may think all slave owners are cruel and brutal. But I was Ford's slave for a long time, and I got to know him well. There was never a kinder, more noble man. The friends, relatives, and influences he grew up with and that were around him all his life, made him blind to the evils of slavery. He spent his life among slaveholders and slaves, and he never thought it was wrong to own, buy, and sell other people. But a slave was lucky to be owned by him.

I spent almost all of the two days it took our ship

to reach the Red River country thinking of ways to escape. Sometimes I almost went up to Ford and told him the truth about myself, and I'm sure now that he would have freed me. But I was afraid. I later learned that a master who knew of my right to freedom would try to get rid of me as fast as a thief gets rid of a stolen horse. I could be sold away even farther south, over the Texas border. So I never told Ford.

We got to Ford's plantation after leaving the boat at the town of Alexandria, Louisiana, took a railroad to the small town of Lamourie, and then walked twelve miles on the Texas Road. It was a very hot day. Harry, Eliza, and I were still weak from the smallpox, and our feet were sore. We walked slowly, and Ford told us to take our time and rest whenever we wanted.

The country around the Red River is low and marshy. The Pine Woods are high ground, by comparison, covered with oak, chestnut, and pine trees. The woods are full of long-horned cattle. Some of them are marked and branded. The rest seem to run wild.

Just as the sun was setting, we came to an opening in the woods, an opening of about twelve acres. In the middle was a two-story house, with a porch in front. In the back was a log kitchen house, a chicken house, corncribs, and a few cabins for slaves. It was a quiet, lonely, pleasant place. It was William Ford's home.

Ford was a wealthy man. Besides his plantation in the Pine Woods, he owned a large lumber company on Indian Creek, four miles away, and also his wife's plantation and many slaves, down the bayou.

As we approached, a girl named Rose stood watching against one of the pillars that held up the roof over the porch. She called her mistress when she saw us coming, and Mrs. Ford came running out, kissed her husband, and asked if he had bought "those niggers."

Ford told us to go around to Sally's cabin and rest ourselves. Sally was around the back washing clothes, and her baby children were rolling in the grass nearby. She took us to her cabin, and told us to lay down our bundles. John, the cook, a boy of about sixteen, came running in, looked us all in the eye, and then ran out again, laughing loudly. Not many strangers came here, it seemed, and he was happy to see us.

We lay down and went to sleep. My thoughts, as usual, were of my wife and children.

After breakfast the next day, a slave named Walton rode into the clearing on a wagon loaded with lumber. Ford sent Harry and me with him to the lumber mill on Indian Creek. We found two more slaves at the mill. We were put to work piling lumber and chopping logs, which we did every day for the rest of the summer.

We usually spent Sundays at the clearing, and our master would gather all his slaves around him and read the Bible to us. Sam, a slave who had been sold to Ford years earlier by Birch, became deeply religious during that summer. Mrs. Ford gave him a Bible, although he could not read well. I read it to him sometimes, and white men who came to visit noticed how religious Sam was. They didn't like it, and they would say that a man like Ford, who gave his slaves Bibles, was "not fit to own a nigger."

But Ford lost nothing by being kind to us. Those who treat their slaves well get the best work out of them. We tried to surprise him at the end of the day with more work than he had asked us to do.

Because I liked to please him, I gave him an idea that made him some profit. He had a contract to deliver lumber to Lamourie, and it had always been delivered by land, which was expensive. Indian Creek was a deep, narrow stream emptying into Bayou Boeuf. In some places it was not more than twelve feet wide and blocked by fallen trees. If the stream could be cleared, the lumber could be shipped cheaper by water.

Adam Taydem, a little white man, was foreman of the mill. He didn't think much of my idea, but Ford thought it was worth a try. I removed the fallen logs, and made a raft—I still remembered how to be a lumberjack from my days on the Champlain Canal.

The arrival of the raft at Lamourie, loaded with lumber, made a sensation. Platt was called "the smartest nigger in the Pine Woods." I was the Robert Fulton of Indian Creek! After that I was in charge of bringing all the lumber out of the woods.

There were still some Chickasaw or Chickopee Indians living in the forest along the creek, and I passed their villages whenever I went down to Lamourie with lumber. They lived in simple huts, ten or twelve feet square, made of pine poles and bark. The Indians lived on deer, raccoon, and opossum, and sometimes they traded the meat for whiskey. Their land stretched west to the Sabine River, and occasionally a tribe from Texas would come over to visit, and there would be a great party in the woods. They were crude but harmless people, worshiped their Great Spirit, loved whiskey, and were happy.

In the fall, I left the mill and was put to work at the clearing. One day, Mrs. Ford asked her husband to buy a loom so that Sally could weave cloth for the slaves' winter clothes. He had no idea where to buy one until I suggested that I make one. I was allowed to go to a nearby plantation to see their loom, and, after a while, built one of my own. Sally said it was perfect; she could weave fourteen yards a day, milk the cows, and have spare time besides. It worked so well that I was put to work making looms for other planters.

At about this time, a carpenter named John Tibeats came to the clearing to do some work on the master's house. I was told to leave the looms and help him. For two weeks, I worked with him, planing and matching boards for a ceiling.

Tibeats was the opposite of Ford in every way. He was a small, crabby, quick-tempered, and spiteful man. He was not respected even by the slaves. During my stay in the Great Pine Woods, I had seen only the bright side of slavery, but, with the coming of Tibeats, the darker side began to open up.

CHAPTER 6

Sold to Tibeats

WILLIAM FORD began to have money troubles. His brother, Franklin Ford, who lived farther upstream, past Alexandria, took out a large loan, and couldn't pay it back. William Ford was forced to pay it for him. And he also owed money to John Tibeats for building the Indian Creek mill for him, and for a weaving house and a corn mill and other unfinished work.

To pay Tibeats and pay off his brother's debt, Ford had to sell eighteen slaves. He sold seventeen, including Sam and Harry, to Peter Compton, a planter on the Red River.

I was sold to Tibeats, probably because of my skill as a carpenter. This was in the winter of 1842. My price was $400 more than Ford owed Tibeats, and Ford took a mortgage for the difference—just like a mortgage on a house.

Tibeats and I left for Mrs. Ford's plantation on

Bayou Boeuf. It is a weak, winding, and sluggish stream, and large cotton and sugar plantations line each bank. It is alive with alligators, who eat the pigs and slave children who are careless enough to wander nearby.

I met Eliza there, for the first time in a month. Mrs. Ford had not been happy with her because Eliza spent so much time sorrowing about her lost children instead of working. She had gotten weak and thin. Her drooping body and hollow cheeks showed that she did not have far to go before she sank entirely.

Ford's overseer on this plantation was a kindly man named Chapin, who came from Pennsylvania. Like everyone else, he had very little use for Tibeats.

As Tibeats's slave, I had to work very hard. From early dawn to late at night, he did not let me have a moment's rest. Tibeats was never satisfied. He never spoke a kind word to anyone. I was his faithful slave and earned him good money, but every night I went to bed with nothing but his curses to show for it.

We finished the corn mill and the kitchen house and were working on an addition to the weaving house, when I committed a crime that can be punished by death in Louisiana.

The weaving house was a few yards from Chapin's house. One night, after I had worked until it was too dark to see, Tibeats ordered me to get up very early the next morning, get a keg of nails from Chapin, and start putting up the siding on the weaving house. I went to bed after talking with Eliza, who was one of the slaves in the cabin I shared. The others were a man called Bristol, another named Lawson, and Lawson's wife, Mary.

Before daylight, I was on Chapin's porch waiting for him to wake up. I didn't dare wake him up myself—no slave would have done that. He came out after a while. Taking off my hat, I told him that Master Tibeats told me to ask him for a keg of nails.

He rolled out a keg, saying, "If Tibeats wants you to use a different size, you can come and get them when I come back later. But use these in the meantime." Then he mounted his horse and rode off into the fields to oversee the slaves.

As day began to break, Tibeats came out, and he seemed even more disagreeable than usual. He may have been my master and owned my flesh and blood, but there was no law that could keep me from looking at him with disgust.

I was working on one side of the house and had just come around to the other side to get some more nails from the keg.

"I thought I told you to start putting up the siding this morning," he growled.

"Yes, master, and I'm doing it," I answered.

"Where?" he demanded.

"On the other side."

He walked around to the other side, looked at my work for a while, and muttered to himself.

"Didn't I tell you last night to get a keg of nails from Chapin?" he burst out at last.

"Yes, master, and I did; and the overseer said he

would get another size for you when he came back, if you wanted it."

Tibeats walked around to the keg, looked in for a moment, and then kicked it over. He came at me violently angry.

"God damn you, I thought you knew something."

"I tried to do as you told me, master. I didn't mean anything wrong. Overseer said—" But he interrupted me with a flood of curses. He ran toward the house and took down one of Chapin's whips. It was three feet long, made of rawhide strips, and loaded with lead at the base.

I knew he intended to whip me, and it was the first time anyone had tried since I came to Louisiana. Besides, I had been faithful and was guilty of nothing but doing the best I could. I should be praised, not whipped. My fear turned to anger, and before he reached me, I decided that I would not be whipped.

He came up to me and ordered me to strip.

"Master Tibeats," I said, looking him in the eye. "I won't." I was about to explain why, when he jumped at me, one hand at my throat and the other raising the whip.

Before he could hit me, I caught him by the coat collar, and drew him close to me. I reached down, grabbed his leg, and pushed him over backward. When he was down, I put my foot on his neck. He was completely in my power, and my blood was up. I snatched the whip in my hands. He struggled with all his strength and swore that I would not live another day, that he would tear my heart out. I don't remember how many times I hit him. After a while, he screamed, and cried murder, and called on God for mercy. But I gave him no mercy, and the whip wrapped around his cringing, wiggling body until my arm ached.

I was too busy to look around me, but, after a while, I noticed Mrs. Chapin looking out the window, and a slave named Rachel standing in the kitchen doorway. Tibeats's screams could be heard in the field, and Chapin was coming as fast as he could ride. I struck Tibeats once again and then pushed him over with a quick kick.

He rose to his feet, brushed the dirt from his hair, and stood looking at me, pale with pain and rage. No one said anything until Chapin rode up, shouting, "What's the matter?"

"Master Tibeats wants to whip me for using the nails you gave me," I blurted out.

"What is the matter with the nails?" he asked, turning to Tibeats.

Tibeats kept looking at me with his snakish eyes flashing in hatred.

"They were a little too large," he said after a while, but never took his eyes away from me.

"I am the overseer here," Chapin began. "I told Platt to take them and use them, and if they were not the right size I would get others later. It is not his fault. Besides, I shall give you whatever nails I please. I hope you understand that, Mr. Tibeats."

Tibeats didn't answer, but he shook his fist at me, ground his teeth, and swore that it was not yet half over. He and Chapin went back to the house, talking in whispers, and I stood there not knowing what was going to happen.

After a while, Tibeats saddled his horse and rode down the road to Cheneyville. Chapin came out, very excited, and told me not to leave the plantation for any reason. He told me not to run—my master was a rascal, and there might be trouble before evening.

I began to realize what I had done. A slave without friends—what could I do, what could I say, in the face of the crime of not taking a white man's insult? For at least an hour I stood there, my anger turning again to fear, when Tibeats rode up with two other horsemen. They rode into the yard, jumped from their horses, and approached me with a large whip and a coil of rope.

"Cross your hands," Tibeats commanded.

"You do not need to tie me up, Master Tibeats. I am ready to go with you anywhere," I answered.

One of the two men stepped up and swore that if I fought back the least little bit, he would break my head, he would tear me limb from limb, he would cut my black heart out. I crossed my hands, and Tibeats tied my wrists together, and then my ankles and then my elbows. It was impossible for me to move. Then he made a noose and put it around my neck.

"Now then, where shall we hang the nigger?" he asked.

One man suggested a nearby tree limb, but the other said it would probably break, and he suggested another.

I said nothing all this time. Chapin was pacing up and down the porch. After a while, as they were dragging me toward the tree, Chapin walked up with a pistol in each hand and said, as best I can remember:

"Gentlemen, I have a very few words to say. You had better listen to them. Whoever moves that slave another foot from here is a dead man. In the first place, he does not deserve this treatment. It is a shame to murder him this way. I never knew a more faithful boy than Platt. You, Tibeats, are at fault. You are pretty much of a scoundrel, and I know it, and you richly deserve the beating you got. In the next place, I have been overseer of this plantation for seven years, and in the absence of William Ford, I am the master here. My duty is to protect his interests. Ford holds a $400 mortgage on that slave, and if you hang him, Ford will lose his money. Until that's paid up, you have no right to take his life. You have no right to take it anyway. There is a law for the slave as well as the white man.

"As for you," he said, turning to the other two men, Cook and Ramsey, overseers of nearby plantations, "as for you—be gone. If you care for your safety, be gone."

Cook and Ramsey, without a word, got on their horses and rode off. Tibeats, after a while, sneaked off like a coward and followed them.

I stayed where I was, with the rope still around my neck. As soon as Tibeats was gone, Chapin called for Lawson and sent him off on a mule as fast as he could.

"Tell Master Ford to come here at once—he must not delay a moment. Tell him they are trying to murder Platt."

Toward noon it began to get unbearably hot. The earth almost blistered people's feet. I was still standing the way Tibeats left me—tied up and without a coat or hat, while big drops of sweat rolled down my face. I could not move an inch because I was tied so tightly. I wanted to lie down, but I knew I would not be able to get up again, and the earth would only make me hotter. My wrists and ankles and the muscles in my arms and legs began to swell.

Chapin spent the day pacing nervously up and down the porch. He didn't go into the fields, and he seemed to expect Tibeats to return with more of his friends. He seemed ready to defend me with his life. I never understood why he didn't untie the ropes. Maybe he wanted Ford to see what Tibeats had almost done to me. Why Tibeats never returned is another mystery, but maybe he thought that in this case discretion would be the better part of valor, as the saying goes.

I was getting weak and hungry, groaning with pain. Only once Rachel dared come up to me with a tin of water, but she was afraid of crossing Chapin. So she left after a sip or two, saying only, "Oh, Platt, how I pity you!"

Just after sunset, Ford came riding into the yard. He had ridden his horse so hard that it was covered with foam. He talked to Chapin for a moment and then came and cut my ropes with a knife.

"Thank God," I said, "Thank God, Master Ford, that you have come at last."

"Poor Platt, you are in a bad state," was all he said.

I tried to walk, but I was so weak that I staggered like a drunken man and fell to my knees. Ford went back to the house. As he reached it, Tibeats and his two friends rode up again. He and Ford argued for a while, and then they left again.

When it got dark, I crawled into the cabin and lay down. I was in great pain, and the slightest movement caused me terrible suffering. After a while, the field hands came in. Eliza and Mary boiled me a piece of bacon and scorched some cornmeal, but I was too weak to eat. They all gathered around me, asking questions. Then Rachel told the whole story, and then Lawson told it over again. They all giggled nervously when Rachel told the part where I kicked Tibeats over. They were fascinated, and afraid, that a slave could fight his master. And amazed that I was still alive.

Suddenly, Chapin came in and told me: "Platt, you will sleep on the floor of the great house tonight; bring your blanket with you."

On the way to Ford's house—the master's or overseer's house was always called "the great house," no matter how big or small it was—he told me that Tibeats might be back before morning, that Tibeats intended to kill me, and that he wanted witnesses if anything happened. If Tibeats stabbed me in front of a hundred slaves, not one of them, by the laws of Louisiana, could come to court and testify against him. The law did not let any slave stand up against a white man for any reason in Louisiana. I lay down on the floor and tried to sleep.

Around midnight, a dog began to bark. Chapin got up and looked out the window, but he couldn't see anything. After a while, the dog stopped barking.

"I think that scoundrel is lurking around somewhere, Platt," Chapin said to me. "If the dog barks again, wake me up."

About an hour later, the dog started barking again, running up to the gate and back again. Chapin was awake in a second, but he still couldn't see anything outside. The dog went back to its kennel, and we went back to sleep. We were not bothered again all night. I'll never know if Tibeats was there that night, but I'm sure he was.

The next morning we were back at work on the weaving house again, and Tibeats never said anything about what had happened. We finished at the end of the week, and Tibeats told me that he was hiring me out to Peter Tanner, Mrs. Ford's brother, to work for a carpenter named Myers. Anything was better than working for Tibeats, so I was happy with the change.

When I got to Tanner's, I found that the story had become famous. Together with my raft on Indian Creek, it was well known that Platt Ford, now Platt Tibeats—a slave's name changes with each new owner—that Platt Tibeats was "a devil of a nigger."

"You're the nigger that beat your master, eh?"

Tanner said when I got there. "You're the nigger that kicks his master and holds him by the legs and hits him, eh? I'd like to see you hold me by the legs. You're a very important character. You're a great nigger, a very remarkable nigger, aren't you! I'd take the tantrums out of you. Just take hold of my leg, if you please, and you'll see! None of your pranks here, boy, remember that. Now go to work, you kicking rascal."

I worked with Myers for a month, and we were both happy about it.

Like Ford, Tanner was in the habit of reading the Bible to his slaves on Sunday. The first Sunday after I arrived, he called us all together and began reading the twelfth chapter of Luke. When he came to the forty-seventh verse, he looked up intently and read:

" 'And that servant which knew his lord's *will,* and prepared not himself, neither did according to his will, shall be beaten with many stripes.' "

"Did you hear that," he demanded. "Stripes."

"That nigger that doesn't take care, that doesn't obey his lord—that's his master—shall be beaten with many stripes. Now 'many' signifies a great many— forty, fifty, a hundred, a hundred and fifty lashes. That's Scripture!" He went on like that for a long time.

At the end of the sermon, he called up three slaves, Warner, Will, and Major, and called me up, too.

"Here, Platt, you held Tibeats by the legs; now I'll see if you can hold these rascals in the same way, until I get back from church meeting."

He ordered them into the stocks, which were common in the Red River country. The stocks were made from two wooden planks, held to posts driven into the ground. There were holes cut in them for legs, and hinges attached so that a slave's legs could be locked between the two, and he could not get out. Often, a slave's neck is put in, instead of his legs, especially when he is being whipped.

Warner, Will, and Major were guilty of melon-stealing. Handing me the key, Tanner, with Mrs. Tanner and Myers, rode away to church in Cheney-ville. While they were gone, the men begged me to let them out. I felt sorry for them, and remembered my own suffering in the sun. I made them promise to return to the stocks later, and then let them out. In return for my kindness—what else could they do?—they led me to the melon patch, where we spent a happy afternoon. They were back in the stocks when Tanner returned.

"Aha! You haven't been out strolling around much today, have you?" he cried. "I'll teach you what's what. I'll teach you not to eat melons on the Lord's day, you Sabbath-breaking niggers."

Peter Tanner was a deacon of the church in Cheneyville, and a very religious man.

CHAPTER 7

Runaway Slave

AFTER A MONTH, I was sent back over the bayou to Tibeats, who was building a cotton press for Ford in a lonely part of the plantation where almost no one ever went. I remembered Chapin's advice to me to beware, because Tibeats might try to kill me at any time. So we worked together, side by side, and I kept one eye on my work and the other on Tibeats. I did my best to give him no reason to complain, to work harder than ever, to take his insults, to take anything but a physical attack.

The third morning after I returned, Chapin left the plantation for an all-day trip to Cheneyville. Tibeats was having one of his really bad days, and his mood was like poison. It was about nine in the morning, and I was busy planing down a piece of wood. Tibeats was working nearby.

"You are not planing down enough," he said, coming over to me.

"It's just even with the line," I answered.

"You're a damned liar," he said angrily.

"Oh, well, master," I said as mildly as I could, "I'll plane it down more if you say so." But before I could plane off one piece, he shouted that I had gone too deeply, that I had spoiled it.

He cursed me bitterly, and I did the best I could to calm him down. But he got angrier and angrier. Finally, he picked up a hatchet from the workbench and ran toward me, swearing he would cut my head open.

It was a moment of life or death. The sharp blade of the hatchet glinted in the sun, and in another second it would be buried in my brain. I had only a second to make up my mind. If I stood still, he would cut my head open. If I ran, he would probably throw it like a knife and hit me in the back. With choices like that, what could I do? I grabbed the hatchet with one hand and his throat with the other. We stood looking at each other for a split second, and I could see murder in his eyes. I would have yelled for help, but Chapin was away, and no one was ever in this part of the plantation.

I brought him down with a sudden kick, grabbed the hatchet, and threw it into the bushes. Frantic with rage, he grabbed a five-foot-long white oak log. Again he rushed at me, and again I met him, picked him up around the waist, and fell on top of him. I threw the log away, too.

Next, he went for an axe that was lying on the workbench. But it was under a heavy piece of wood, and while he was struggling with it, I sprang on his back and pressed him down so that he couldn't move. We rested in that position for a few moments, and then I tried to pull the axe away. I couldn't, and did the next best thing—I grabbed him around the throat and squeezed. He became weak and stopped fighting. His face, which had been pale with rage, was turning blue and black from suffocation. There was a devil in me that told me to kill him while I had the chance. But I began to realize the spot I was in. If I killed him, I would be hanged for murder. If I let him live, nothing would stop him from killing me.

So, twice within a few moments, I had choices that meant life or death. I threw him to the ground and ran.

I leaped over a nearby fence, ran across the fields, and plunged into a thick wood and hid there. I climbed a fence to look back for a second, and I could see Tibeats saddling his horse and riding away. I rested, but in less than an hour, some of the slaves I had passed in the fields began shouting for me to run. Tibeats and two other men came riding up with a pack of bloodhounds. The bloodhounds used for slave-hunting in Bayou Boeuf are particularly savage, much more than those in the North. They will attack a black man and cling to him as if he were a wounded deer—I never knew a slave to escape with his life from Bayou Boeuf. One reason is that slaves are not allowed to learn how to swim, and can't cross the smallest stream. Whichever way they run in this part of the country, they can't go far without hitting water. And then they can choose between drowning and the dogs. It was a good thing for me that I had learned how to swim well as a boy in New York.

I jumped down from the fence and ran as fast as I could. The dogs were gaining on me, and they were yelping and howling as they ran. I expected to feel them jumping on my back any second and sink their teeth into my flesh. At last I came to water. It was only a few inches deep, but soon it went up over my ankles, then my knees and then over my waist. I could hear the dogs falling farther and farther behind me. They must have been confused. I kept running and finally came to a big, wide bayou—the Pacoudrie Bayou. The water carried the smell of me away, and even the best bloodhound could not follow me now.

I swam through the bayou and plunged into the Great Pacoudrie Swamp on the other side. It is filled for thirty or forty miles with giant sycamore, gum, cottonwood, and cypress trees. No one lives in it, except bears, wildcats, panthers, and thousands of big, slimy alligators. And hundreds of deadly water moccasin snakes. Every log, every fallen tree limb was covered with them. They crawled away from me, but sometimes I almost stepped on them. Their bite has more poison than a rattlesnake's, and they give no warning.

The noise I made splashing through the water usually scared off the alligators, but sometimes I would come right up to one without seeing him. And then I would have to jump back and circle around him. They can run straight forward at a good speed, but they have difficulty moving sideways, and they are easy to beat in a crooked race.

I heard the last of the dogs at about two in the afternoon. Probably they never crossed the bayou. But I kept going all afternoon and night. I was more careful now—before stepping in a puddle, I would hit the water with a stick. If something in the water moved, I'd walk around it. If not, I'd walk through it.

I kept moving all night, more afraid of the alligators and snakes than of anyone chasing me. The moon rose above the trees, giving me some light, and I decided that I had better try to reach Master Ford's house in the Great Pine Woods. I couldn't stay in the swamp, that was certain, and there was no going back to Tibeats.

My clothes were in tatters, and my hands, face, and body were covered with scratches. My feet were stuck full of thorns, and I was smeared with muck and the green slime that collects on the dead water of a swamp. At last I reached the Pacoudrie Bayou again and swam it. Just as dawn broke, I reached dry land. I was sure I was in the Great Pine Woods.

As the sun came up, I reached a small clearing I had never seen before. At the edge of the woods, a young master and a slave were catching wild hogs. I knew the white man would ask to see a pass from my master that would let me move around far from home. He would take me to jail if I couldn't show one. I was too tired to run away from him. So I decided to try another way.

I put on the meanest expression I could and walked

right up to him, staring him in the eyes. He looked frightened and moved backward when he saw me—I must have looked like a spirit come up out of hell.

"Where does William Ford live?" I demanded.

"He lives seven miles from here," the white man answered.

"Which is the way to his place?" I demanded, trying to look meaner than before.

"Do you see those trees?" he asked. "Well, at the feet of those pine trees runs the Texas Road. Turn to the left, and it will lead you to William Ford's."

Without another word, I hurried ahead, happy as he was to put as much distance as I could between us. At about eight o'clock, I reached Ford's house.

Stepping up to the porch, I knocked on the door, which was opened by Mrs. Ford. I must have looked frightening. I asked for Ford, and he came out in a moment. I told him everything that had happened, and he listened quietly, with a kind look on his face. He took me into the kitchen and called John, who gave me some food. I had not eaten anything since the morning before.

I slept late into the afternoon, when I awoke very stiff and sore. After eating again, I started trimming the rose bushes in Mrs. Ford's garden and clearing out the weeds in the peach and orange trees. It was late fall, but in that part of the country, the flowers and fruit bloom and ripen all year long. I was trying to show my thanks. Mrs. Ford came out and told me that I didn't have to work, but I kept at it for three days.

On the fourth day, Ford ordered me to come with him up the bayou. He rode his horse, and I trotted alongside. I left that little clearing in the Pine Woods with regret and sadness. For years to come, I would think of it as an oasis in the desert, a little paradise. Ford wanted me to change places with him from time to time, but I said that it was better for me to walk than for him, and I kept trotting along for a few hours. We were less than five miles from the plantation, when Tibeats came riding up in the distance. He looked at me for only a second, and then turned his horse around and rode alongside Ford, talking quietly. I trotted along behind.

"Well," I heard Tibeats tell Ford. "I never saw such running before. I'll bet him against a hundred dollars, he'll beat any nigger in Louisiana. I offered John David Cheney twenty-five dollars to catch him, dead or alive, but he outran his dogs in a fair race. Those Cheney dogs aren't much, anyway, but somehow they got off the track, and we had to give up the hunt. We rode the horses as far as we could, and then kept up on foot until the water was three feet deep. The boys said he was drowned, for sure. I sure wanted to get a shot at him. Ever since, I've been riding up and down the bayou, but didn't have much hope of catching him—I thought for sure he was dead. Oh, he can run, that nigger can."

He kept up that way for a long while. When he finished Ford began by saying that Platt had always been a faithful boy with him and that he was sorry we had had such trouble, and that according to Platt's story, he had been treated badly. It was a shame to use hatchets and axes on slaves, he said, and no one should be allowed to do it.

"A little kindness would be far more useful in restraining them, and making them obey, than the use of such deadly weapons. It is evident, Mr. Tibeats, that you and Platt cannot live together. You dislike him and would not hesitate to kill him, and he knows it and will run from you in fear of his life. Now, Tibeats, you must sell him or hire him out. Unless you do, I will take legal measures to get him out of your possession."

And Ford kept up that way for a long while. I kept my mouth shut. When we reached the plantation, I was sent to Eliza's house, where all the slaves were astonished to find me alive.

That night, they all gathered around me again to hear about my new adventure. They took it for granted that I would be whipped, and that it would be hard—500 lashes is usually what a slave got for running away.

"Poor fellow," Eliza said, taking my hand. "It would have been better if you had drowned. You have a cruel master and he will kill you yet."

Lawson said that Chapin might be told to give the whipping, and then it would be lighter. The others hoped it would be Ford, for then there would be no whipping at all.

Early in the morning, Tibeats left the plantation. But in the morning, a tall, good-looking man came up to me and asked if I was Tibeats's boy—all male slaves are called boy, even old ones. I took off my hat and said that I was.

"How would you like to work for me?" he asked.

"Oh, I'd like to, very much," I answered. Anything was better than Tibeats.

"You worked under Myers at Tanner's, didn't you? Well, I have hired you to work for me in the Big Cane Brake thirty-eight miles from here down the Red River."

His name was Eldret, and he lived below Ford's on the same side of the bayou. The next morning, I went with him and his slave Sam and a wagonload of supplies drawn by four big mules to the Big Cane Brake.

After crossing the Bayou Rouge Swamp, we entered the cane brake and followed a little-used road, barely wide enough for the wagon. The cane there is the kind used for fishing rods, and it grows so thick together that a man standing a few feet away can't be seen between. The tracks of bears and panthers crossed our trail, and alligators swarmed in puddles of cloudy water.

We kept on until we came to Sutton's Field. Many years ago a criminal named Sutton came here, running away from the law, and built a house and lived like a hermit. One day the Indians came and massacred him, or so the story goes. For miles around, in the slave quarters and wherever the white children gather to listen to stories of ghosts and witches, the story goes that Sutton's Field is haunted. For more than twenty-five years, hardly anyone had come here.

Weeds grew in the abandoned fields, and snakes sunned themselves on the crumbling porch of the old house. It was an awful place.

Soon we reached Eldret's land. We went to work with our cane knives and cleared enough space to build two cabins. We cut down trees, split them into boards, and built the cabins, using leaves for the roofs.

The great problem was the flies. They flew into our mouth, eyes, ears, and nose, and dug under our skin. They seemed set on eating us up alive, and there was nothing we could do. I never knew a more lonely or more ugly spot. Yet, for me it was a pleasure, since Tibeats was far away.

After a few days, four big, heavy black girls came and took over the work of cutting down the trees. In fact, around the Bayou Boeuf, women were used for all sorts of heavy work, such as ploughing, driving teams, clearing wild land, and working on highways. Some planters had nothing but women slaves.

When we first arrived at the cane brake, Eldret promised me that if I worked well, he would let me visit my friends at Ford's in four weeks. At the fifth week, I reminded him of his promise, and he told me that I had done well and could go.

But Tibeats came there that day and, when he heard that I was going to visit friends, he said: "It isn't worthwhile. The nigger will get unsteady. He can't go."

But Eldret said that I had worked well, and that he had promised, and said that I could go. At daybreak, I was at his door, waiting for a pass. But it was Tibeats who came out—in one of his bad moods. With no patience left in me for this man, I started on my way.

"Are you going without a pass?" he growled.

"Yes, master," I said, stopping. "I thought I would."

"How do you think you'll get there?"

"Don't know," was all I said.

"You'll be taken and sent to jail, where you ought to be, before you get halfway," he said, and went in to write a pass. He came out with the pass in his hand, muttering, "Damned nigger deserves a hundred lashes." And he threw it to the ground. I picked it up and hurried away.

A slave caught off his master's plantation without a pass can be taken and whipped by any white man he meets. On the way, a lot of people asked me for my pass. Those who looked like gentlemen never even looked at me, but poor white men never let the chance go by. Catching runaway slaves is a money-making business. After they have advertised that one has been caught, if no one comes to claim him, they can sell him to the highest bidder. And if the slave's master comes for him, the master has to pay a fee.

There are no restaurants in that part of the state. I had no money and carried no food, but I was never hungry. All a slave had to do was show his pass to the nearest planter, and he would be sent around to the back for food and shelter. No matter what faults they had, the people of the Red River country did have hospitality.

I arrived at Ford's in the late afternoon and spent the evening with Eliza, Lawson, and Rachel. When we had left Washington, Eliza was plump and healthy. She stood tall in her silks and jewels. Now she was thin and haggard, and she was bowed down. I never saw her afterward. She became useless in the cotton fields and was sold cheaply to another planter, who whipped her all the time. At last, she was helpless. She could not walk, and she lay on her cabin floor for days, grieving for her lost children. Her master let her lie there, and one day, the hands returning from the field found her dead on the floor. She was free at last!

I set out to go back to the cane brake the next day and met Tibeats on the road. He told me not to go farther than the next plantation, since he had just sold me to its owner, Edwin Epps.

I was free of Tibeats. I was no longer his dog, and it was a relief when I delivered myself to my new owner.

Tibeats disappeared from that part of the state soon afterward. I saw him once later, when I was passing through a distant town in a slave gang. He was sitting in a cheap saloon, and I don't think he saw me.

CHAPTER 8

Epps's Cotton Plantation

EDWIN EPPS is a large, heavy man with a sharp expression. His language is vulgar, and I've often seen him drunk, sometimes for two weeks at a time. But lately he has gotten better, and when I left him, he didn't drink at all. But when he was drunk, he would love to dance with his slaves or whip them just to hear them shriek and cry.

He had been an overseer on another man's plantation when he was younger, but now he rented a plantation on Bayou Huff Power, about twelve miles from Cheneyville. His main crop was cotton, and it was here that I first learned how most of the slaves in the South spend their lives:

They plant the cotton seeds in March or April, and the plants begin to appear about a week afterward. Then the hoeing starts. An overseer on a horse drives the slaves forward, and the fastest hoer takes the lead row. If any of the others passes him, he is whipped. If one falls behind for a moment, that slave is whipped. In fact, the whip is used all day long.

Each field is hoed again and again until August, when the picking season begins. Each slave is given a sack, with a strap, which hangs from his neck. When a new slave is sent into the fields for the first time, he is whipped up properly and made to pick as fast as he can the first day. At night his pickings are weighed, and every night after that he must bring in the same weight. If he falls short, he is whipped. An ordinary day's work is about 200 pounds. An experienced slave who brings back less would be whipped. One slave, a woman named Patsey, was the best for miles around and could pick 500 pounds a day. Slaves are also whipped if they break branches off the cotton plants, since it hurts the plants.

The slaves must be in the fields as soon as it is light in the morning. And except for ten or fifteen minutes at noon to eat their cold bacon and corn-meal, they are never allowed to rest until it is too dark to see.

No matter how tired a slave may be at the end of the day, he never goes to the millhouse without fear. Here the cotton is weighed. If he did not pick enough that day, he knows he will be whipped. If he picked more than expected, he will have to pick that much more every day from then on. Usually, they have less than the standard, and that is why they are never in a hurry to leave the fields, even when it is dark. After the weighings come the beatings, and, even then, the day's work is not over. Each slave still has a chore to do, such as feeding the mules or pigs, cutting wood, or packing cotton. Late at night, they are allowed to go to their cabins, where they cook the next day's meal and then go to sleep.

All they can have is bacon and cornmeal. That and a small amount of salt was all I had to eat at Epps's for ten years. He fed his hogs shelled corn, so that they would grow fatter faster, but he fed us corn on the cob, and we had to shell and grind it ourselves. He was afraid that we might become too fat to work well.

By the time the dinner is cooked, it is usually midnight. Now the slaves can go to sleep, but that too is full of fear. Oversleeping in the morning can be punished by twenty lashes. So the slave goes to sleep with a prayer that he will be on his feet at the first sound of the overseer's horn.

The cabin he sleeps in is made of logs, with no windows, since the cracks between the logs let in plenty of light as well as rain and wind. My bed for all those years was a plank twelve inches wide and ten feet long, and my pillow was a stick of wood.

In the morning, the slave grabs the food he has prepared for the day and runs at the first sound of the horn. It is serious to be found at the cabin after daybreak. And so another day of fear and suffering begins, fear of being caught lagging, fear of picking too much or too little, fear of oversleeping. That is all a slave's life is during the cotton season.

Epps was considered a small planter, since he did not have enough slaves to need an overseer. Larger estates, with fifty or a hundred or two hundred slaves, must have one overseer or more. They ride on horseback armed with pistols, bowie knives, whips, and a pack of dogs. They follow the slaves and keep a sharp lookout. All a man needs for the job is no heart at all. It is his job to see that the crop is as large as it can be, no matter how much suffering must go into each bale of cotton. The dogs are used to catch any slave who tries to run after being whipped too much. The pistols are for any emergency. Even a slave, goaded by the whip, will sometimes turn on the overseer or master.

The gallows still stand at Marksville, the county seat, where a slave was hanged last winter for killing his overseer. He had been told to spend the day splitting rails. But before he could start work, he was sent on another errand, which took up the whole day. The next day he was whipped for not splitting the rails. The slave and the overseer were alone in the woods, and the slave let himself be whipped as long as he could. Finally, the pain and injustice of it made him jump up, grab an axe, and cut his overseer to pieces. He confessed to his master right away and was hanged immediately.

Besides the overseers, there are drivers, or assistant overseers, who are slaves themselves. They have to do their share of the work and whip the other slaves as well. When a slave stops sweating, as he often does when overworked, many times he will just fall to the ground. Then the driver has to drag him to the shade, throw buckets of water over him, and force him back to work.

At the plantation on Bayou Huff Power, Tom was the driver when I first came. After we moved to Bayou Boeuf, I was given that awful job for eight years. I never dared show much mercy, for I soon learned that wherever Epps was, he was watching us. If one of us was slow or not busy during the day, we would hear about it when we came back. It was a matter of principle with him to punish any offense he noticed. The offender was punished, and so was I for permitting it.

If, on the other hand, he had seen me use the whip a lot, he was satisfied. In those eight years, I learned to use the whip well, and I was able to throw the lash within a fraction of an inch of a slave's neck, ear, face, or back. If we saw Epps coming, or thought that he was sneaking around, I would start to whip at them as if I meant it. And, according to our agreement, they would squirm and scream as if in agony, although I never touched them at all. Patsey would, when she could, tell Epps that Platt whipped them cruelly all day, and old Abram would say that Platt whipped them worse than General Andrew Jackson whipped the British at the Battle of New Orleans. If Epps wasn't drunk, that was enough to satisfy him. If he was drunk, someone had to suffer, no matter what.

The only rest from constant work that a slave has throughout the whole year is during the Christmas holidays. Epps allowed us three days, while other planters sometimes allowed more. It is the only time that the slaves look forward to all year. They are glad when night comes, not only because the day's work is over, but because it brings them closer to Christ-mas.

The holidays are a time of feasting and frolicking and fiddling. They are the only days when the slaves are allowed a little liberty, and they make the most of it. Each year, a different planter in the neighbor-hood usually gives a "Christmas supper" for all the slaves nearby. Three or four hundred slaves come from all around, dressed in their best clothes. The cotton coats are washed, the shoes are shined, and, if they are lucky enough to own a discarded hat with-out a rim or without a crown, they wear that proudly. The women, who usually wear bandanas around their heads, wear scarves or ribbons if they have them.

A table is spread outdoors and loaded with all sorts of meats and vegetables—no more bacon and cornmeal. White people come just to see the slaves eat and be happy.

After the meal, the next order of business is danc-ing, and I was always asked to play my violin. Epps often received letters as far away as ten miles, asking him to send me over to play at some party or dance the whites were giving. I always returned with some coins in my pockets, and when young white people would see me walking around, they would always ask: "Where are you going, Platt? What's happening tonight?"

During the rest of the holiday, the slaves are given passes and allowed to go wherever they want, or they can stay on the plantation and work for wages, but almost no one ever does. They can be seen hurrying in all directions, smiling and happy. They visit, see old friends, and sometimes even get married.

Marriage, of course, is not real marriage, since there is no real marriage among slaves. The only ceremony needed is the consent of the owners. Either person can have as many husbands or wives as the owner allows, and can end the marriage whenever they like. If the wife does not live on the same plantation, the husband is permitted to visit her on Saturday night, if it isn't too far away. Abram had a wife seven miles away, but he was getting old and had pretty much forgotten her. The children of such a marriage, of course, belong not to the father or the mother, but to the mother's master. The owners try to get their women slaves married, boast of their good "breeders," and relish the thought of getting another slave without having to pay for him.

When I arrived at Epps's for the first time, it was hoeing season. I lasted most of the season, but then began to get sick. I had chills and fever, but I wasn't allowed to leave my row. Even when I was healthy, I couldn't keep up with the others, but now I was beaten all the time for falling back, and, after a while, I got so sick that the whip had no effect on me. Finally, around September, when the cotton-picking season began, I was unable to leave my cabin or even walk. The only help I got was from the old cook, who would visit me occasionally and cook food for me.

One day, Epps began to fear that I was dying, so he sent for Dr. Wines, since he didn't want to lose a

$1,000 slave. I got better slowly, and, one day before I was well again, Epps came to the cabin door and ordered me into the fields. I had no experience picking cotton, and, by the end of the day, I had only 95 pounds instead of 200. Epps was furious, and was going to whip me badly, but finally decided not to because it was my first day. But I never got much better—I didn't have the skill of Patsey's quick fingers and hands.

Practice and whipping did no good, and Epps, giving up at last, swore that I was a disgrace, and not fit to associate with "cotton-picking niggers." So I was set to work at other chores, such as cutting and hauling wood, and whatever else needed doing.

It was a rare day that passed without one or more whippings. The poor victim was stripped and forced to lie on the ground, face down, in order to be beaten. The crack of the whip and the shriek of the slaves was heard from sunup to sundown every day.

The number of lashes depends on the reason for the whipping. Twenty-five is considered light, and was ordered, when, for example, a dry leaf or cotton boll was found among the cotton. One hundred was called severe—that was the punishment for standing idle in the fields. One hundred and fifty or 200 was the penalty for quarreling with your cabin-mates, and 500 was the penalty for running away.

Epps was in the habit of coming home drunk from Holmesville, about two and a half miles away, at least every other week. Often, he would break chairs, dishes, and whatever furniture he could lay his hands on. Finished with amusing himself in the house, he would grab his whip and go after the slaves. The first one who came within range was lashed. Sometimes he would keep us running in all directions for hours, dodging corners, and hiding behind the cabins. He was delighted if he could sneak up behind a slave and give him a well-placed blow. The younger children and the old men and women suffered the most. In the midst of all the running, shouting, and confusion, sometimes he would hide behind a cabin, waiting with his whip raised to hit the first black face peering cautiously around a corner.

At other times he would be less brutal, and then he would want us all to dance and laugh. All of us were assembled in the living room of the great house when Epps came home in one of his dancing moods. I would have to play the violin, and Epps would shout, "Dance, you damned niggers, dance!"

Then we all had to step lightly and brightly. "Up and down, heel and toe, and away we go," Epps would shout, and those who weren't lively enough would get a taste of the whip. When he was exhausted, there would be a short pause, and then it was back to dancing. If my tune wasn't lively enough, I would get whipped, too. Mrs. Epps often scolded him, and threatened to go back home to her father, but sometimes she enjoyed herself as much as he did. Many times we had to dance until dawn, and then go into the fields without any sleep. And if we didn't do enough work that day, we were whipped as much as if we had had a good night's sleep.

There was just one crueler man on the bayou, and that was Jim Burns, whose plantation was worked only by women. He kept their backs red and raw.

Epps bought the plantation on Bayou Boeuf two years after he bought me, and we moved in after Christmas in 1845. He took with him nine slaves. Besides me and Uncle Abram and Patsey, there was Wiley and Phebe, Bob, Henry, Edward, and Susan.

Patsey was twenty-three years old and she was slim, straight, and pretty. There was a pride about her that work, beatings, and weariness could not destroy. She could leap the highest fences, outrun the fastest dogs, manage the toughest mule teams, and ride almost any horse. She turned a good furrow when she plowed and was the best at splitting rails. And she was the best cotton-picker for miles around. She was queen of the field.

She was friendly and joyous and lighthearted. Yet, she cried more than all of us together. On her back were the marks of a thousand lashes, not because she wouldn't work or was slow, but because her master could not keep away from her, and his wife was jealous.

In the great house, there would be shouting and arguing and scolding over her for days, and nothing delighted Mrs. Epps more than seeing Patsey suffer. If she tried to resist Epps, he would use his whip on her; if she was not careful when she was around the yard, a piece of wood or a bottle would hit her in the face: Mrs. Epps had good aim. And when Epps was feeling guilty, Mrs. Epps sometimes convinced him to whip Patsey for nothing in particular.

Poor Patsey was caught between them, and Epps refused to sell her. She often begged me to kill her and bury her in the swamp, since that was the only way she would ever escape.

CHAPTER 9

Slavery in the Bayou

THE CATERPILLARS destroyed the cotton crop in 1845, the first year at Epps's new plantation. There was little for the slaves to do, and so when the rumor came to Bayou Boeuf that wages were high, and workers were needed on the sugar plantations in St. Mary's Parish, near the Gulf of Mexico, a number of planters decided to hire out their slaves.

So in September, 147 of us were gathered together in Holmesville, including Abram, Bob, and me. About half were women. Epps, Alonson Pierce, Henry Doler, and Addison Roberts were chosen by the other planters to herd us down to the sugar plantations.

I was hired out to Judge William Turner, who has a plantation on Bayou Sale, a few miles from the Gulf. For a while, I was put to work repairing his sugarhouse. And then a cane knife was put in my hands, and I was sent into the fields. I had no trouble keeping up with the others, the way I did picking cotton. Cutting sugarcane seemed to suit me. After a while, Judge Turner transferred me to the sugarhouse as a driver, and gave me a whip to use on any slave who wasn't busy for even a moment. During the cane-cutting season, the grinding and boiling of the cane into sugar goes on all day and night. Every moment is valuable. If I did not use the whip enough, it was used on me.

It is the custom in Louisiana, and, I suppose, in the other slave states as well, to let a slave keep whatever he earns on Sunday. Since a slave is never given anything except a blanket when he is bought or kidnapped, this is the only way to earn money to buy a knife, a pot, a fork, or a dish.

Since there is not a moment to lose during the cane season on a sugar plantation, everyone worked on Sunday, as they did on a cotton plantation at the height of the cotton-picking. So while we had no choice about working, we were also paid for it that one day a week. I was at Judge Turner's until January, and between that and a party on a nearby plantation, where I was paid for playing my violin, I earned almost ten dollars. I was considered a millionaire by the others. I loved to count the money over and over again, and think of all the things I could buy—coats and hats and shoes and water pails and furniture for the cabin—I was the wealthiest slave on Bayou Boeuf.

One day when I had some free time, I got up the courage to go over to the Rio Teche, a large river nearby, and ask a steamer captain, who sounded like a Northerner, to hide me in his ship and take me north. He pitied me, but said that it would be impossible to get me past the customs officials in New Orleans, and that he would be punished and his ship would be taken away. I was sure he would have helped me if he could have.

The next summer, the caterpillars stayed out of the cotton, but the worms got into the bacon. None of us would eat it, no matter how hungry we were. Whenever we ran out of bacon, we had to hunt in the woods for raccoon and opossum, or else go hungry. But we had to do it last thing at night, after all our chores were done, and we had to use sticks, since slaves are not allowed to have guns. There are plantations where the slaves have no other meat for months at a time.

You can eat raccoon meat, but opossum is the best meat there is, better than beef or pork or veal or anything. Opossums are tricky and clever creatures. If you hit them even lightly, they will roll over on the ground and play dead. If you then run after another one, without first stopping to break the first one's neck, he won't be there when you come back. The little animal has outwitted you—he has played 'possum.

But after eighteen hours of picking cotton and doing chores besides, I had no energy for hunting. My cabin was only a few feet from the bank of the bayou, and I decided that it would be easiest to get food out of the bayou, easier than hunting all night for it. I built a fish trap, which many slaves in that part of the country have since copied. It was made of wooden slats, with a trap door and bait, and the fish who came in after the bait soon found the door closed behind him. All I had to do was come and empty the trap and reset it for the next day.

About this time, something happened in the neighborhood that made a deep impression on me. It also shows something about the people living there. On the other side of the bayou, there was a plantation owned by a man named Marshall. One day, a man from Natchez, Mississippi, came to talk to Marshall about buying the plantation, and later in the day a messenger came running up to us, saying that there was a bloody battle going on and we had better hurry over fast.

We raced over to Marshall's house and found the man from Natchez lying on the floor, covered with blood. He was dead. Marshall stood over him, shouting and cursing and pacing back and forth. Somehow, they had argued over the price, and drawn their guns. Marshall was never arrested, and, although there was some kind of trial, he was not found guilty. He returned to the plantation even more respected than before.

Epps took Marshall's side and went around justifying him to the other planters, but that did not stop Marshall from trying to kill him later. They fought over a game of cards one night, and Marshall rode up to the house one day armed with a knife and pistols, challenging Epps to settle the argument once and for all. Epps stayed in the house that day, not because he was a coward, or because of his conscience, but only because of his wife. But later they became friends again.

This sort of thing went on all the time down there. In the North it would have landed them all in jail, but there no one seemed to notice. I thought about it for a long while, and realized that being slave owners had brutalized them as much as their slaves. They see suffering every day—slaves whipped, beaten, attacked by dogs—how could they not become hardened? There are many kind-hearted men on the bayou, like William Ford, but there are many more who grow up with brutality, and hardly notice it anymore. They are even playful about it, as the following episode will show.

Epps was away at a shooting match in Holmesville one day, and none of us noticed him when he returned. I was hoeing alongside of Patsey when she said to me in a low voice, "Platt, do you see Old Hog Jaw beckoning for me to come to him?"

Looking sideways, I saw Epps, or Old Hog Jaw as we called him, standing at the edge of the field, motioning and making faces. He was drunk. Patsey understood what he wanted, and she began to cry. I whispered to her not to look up, and to continue working, as if she had not seen him. But soon he came staggering over and walked up to me very angry.

"What did you say to Pats?" he demanded. I said something that didn't really answer him.

"How long have you owned this plantation, you damned nigger?" he demanded, sneering and grabbing hold of my shirt collar. "Now I'll cut your black throat, that's what I'll do," he swore, drunk and trying to draw his knife. I jumped away from him, leaving my ripped shirt in his hand.

It was easy to keep away from him after that, since he was very drunk. He chased me until he was out of breath, and then he ordered me to come closer, and he tried to talk me into coming closer. We ran around the field a few times this way, and, after a while, it was more funny than frightening. I knew that when he got sober again, he would laugh at it as much as I would.

After a while, I saw Mrs. Epps coming, and I ran toward her. Epps chased me, but, when he saw his wife, he stopped and stood in the field for almost an hour while I stood next to Mrs. Epps and told her what had happened. Now she was angry, cursing Epps and Patsey about the same amount. Finally, Epps walked up to her, nearly sober now and trying to look innocent as a child. Mrs. Epps began to scold him, and demanded to know why he wanted to cut my throat. He made believe that he was amazed, and swore that he had not said a word to me all day.

"Platt, you lying nigger, have I?" he asked me. Since it is not safe to argue with a master, even by telling the truth, I didn't say anything. The whole thing was never mentioned again.

Shortly afterward, something happened that almost gave away my real name and history. Soon after Epps had bought me, he asked me if I could read and write. I told him I could, and he swore that if he ever found me with a pen and a piece of paper, he would give me a hundred lashes. He bought slaves to work, not to educate, he said. He never asked about my past, but Mrs. Epps often asked me a lot of questions about Washington, because she thought I came from there. And more than once she said that I did not talk or act like the other slaves, and that she was sure that I had seen more of the world than I told about.

I had always hoped to send a letter to my family in New York State since that first letter on the ship, but, in nine years as a slave, I never came across a piece of paper. Even if I had, how could I mail it? I didn't have a pass to go to town, and the postmaster would never mail a letter from a slave without written instructions from that slave's owner.

One day, Mrs. Epps sent me to Holmesville to buy some things, including writing paper, and I stole a sheet on the way home. After trying different ways for a while, I finally managed to make some ink, and made a pen out of a duck feather. I wrote a long letter to a friend in Sandy Hill.

I kept the letter quite a while, hoping to find a way to send it north. After a long time, a man named Armsby, a stranger, came to Epps looking for a job as an overseer, and then applied to the other planters. He stayed with Shaw, who had made a wife of his slave Harriet, and was raising a household of mulattoes. After a time, Armsby ran so short of money that he had to work in the fields with the slaves—a very rare sight in the South. I made the most of every chance I got to talk to him, and, finally, I asked him to mail a letter for me, not daring to tell him that it was already written. And if he couldn't do it, I begged him not to tell Epps. Well, he told me that he could mail it, and that he would never tell Epps. I had the letter in my pocket all the time, but I didn't dare give it to him. I said I'd get it written in a few days.

The next day, Epps sat down on the fence between Shaw's place and his, watching us work. Armsby came over to him and they talked a bit. That night Epps came to my cabin with his whip in his hand.

"Well, boy," he said, "I understand I've got a learned nigger that writes letters and tries to get white fellows to mail them. Wonder if you know who he is?"

My worst fear had come true. I had to think of some good lies fast.

"Don't know anything about it, Master Epps," I said. "Don't know anything about it at all, sir."

"Haven't you asked that fellow, Armsby, to mail a letter for you at Marksville?"

"Why, lord, master, I never spoke three words to him in all my life. I don't know what you mean."

"Well," he continued, "Armsby told me today that the devil is among my slaves; that I had one who needs close watching or he'll run away. And when I asked him why, he said you wanted him to carry a letter to Marksville. What have you got to say to that, eh?"

"All I've got to say, master, is that there is no truth

in it. How could I write a letter without any ink or paper? There is nobody I could want to write to, because I haven't got any friends living anywhere. That Armsby is a lying, drunken fellow, they say, and nobody believes him, anyway. You know I always tell the truth, and I never go off the plantation without a pass. Now, master, I can see what that Armsby is after, plain enough. Didn't he want you to hire him as an overseer?"

"Yes, he wanted me to hire him."

"That's it," I said. "He wants to make you believe we're all going to run away, and then he thinks you'll hire an overseer to watch us. He just made that story up, because he wants a job. It's all a lie, master, you can depend on it."

Epps thought a while, impressed, and finally said, "I'm damned, Platt, if I don't believe you tell the truth. He must take me for a soft one, to think he can give me that kind of a story. Maybe he thinks he can fool me. Maybe he thinks I don't know anything, can't take care of my own slaves, eh? Old Soft Soap Epps, eh? Ha, ha, damned Armsby, set the dogs on him!" And he went on like that for a while and left. As soon as he was gone, I threw the letter, which I'd waited nine years to write, into the fire.

CHAPTER 10

Thoughts of Escape

IN TWELVE YEARS, you might think that one, at least one, chance to escape might come by. But it was impossible. Not a day went by that I didn't think of escaping and plot some scheme. But I always learned from what happened to other slaves who had tried and always failed.

Wiley, Aunt Phebe's shy, quiet husband, tried once, and he never tried again. One night, he sneaked over to another plantation and spent such a happy evening talking and singing softly with his friends that he forgot about the time, and, before he knew it, it was getting light. He ran home as fast as he could, but he was caught by the patrollers.

I don't know about other parts of the South, but in Louisiana, the planters hire men to patrol up and down the roads at night. Their job is to catch, whip, and return any slave out at night without a pass, and even to shoot if he resists. They ride heavily armed and accompanied by dogs, and you can hear the clatter of their horses' hooves all night. And sometimes you can see them driving a slave in front of them or leading him by a rope around his neck.

Wiley ran away from the patrollers, hoping to get to his cabin before they caught him. But a big dog bit into his leg and dragged him down. The patrollers whipped him badly, and Epps whipped him even worse. He was sore, stiff, and miserable for days, and was unable to keep up with the others in hoeing his row. So he was whipped all day for falling behind. Wiley did not have much of a temper, but the whippings became too much for him, and he decided to run away for good. He cooked a whole week's food and ran off on a Sunday evening without even telling his wife.

Epps searched for him everywhere, in the cabins, in the corncrib, in the cotton house, everywhere. He raved and ranted, especially when the dogs were led into the swamps but couldn't pick up his trail. They circled around in the forest, noses to the ground, but never found a trace. Wiley had escaped, we thought, and we were all glad for him.

But he came back about three weeks later.

Later, he told us that he had tried to make it back to South Carolina, where he was raised. He hid in the trees during the day and traveled through the swamp at night. Finally, just before dawn one morning, he reached the Red River. But before he could cross it, a white man came by and asked him for his pass. Of course, he had none, so he was taken to the jail in Alexandria, and, a few days later, Mrs. Epps's uncle came by, recognized him, and reclaimed him.

He gave Wiley a pass and a note to Epps, urging Epps not to whip him, but Epps paid no attention to that. And poor Wiley got the usual 500 lashes. He never tried again.

I *did* get myself ready in some ways for escaping, just in case. I never lost a chance to beat and whip Epps's dogs. Whenever we went hunting for opossum and raccoon, deep in the woods, I would beat them until they crawled away with their tails hanging down between their legs. I'm sure that if they were ever sent after me they would never attack—they were too afraid of me.

No matter how impossible it was to escape, the swamps were always full of starving, half-crazy runaways. Many were sick or worn out and unable to work when they escaped, and they managed to survive a week or two in the swamps before returning to their masters, begging to be forgiven. Anything for a day or two of rest.

While I belonged to Ford, I gave away the hiding place of six or eight runaways who lived in the Great Pine Woods. Not that I wanted to give them away, but I had no choice. I was walking along the Texas Road one night on an errand, carrying a butchered pig over my shoulder. I heard footsteps behind me, and saw two black men coming up behind me fast. When they got close, one raised a club and the other grabbed the pig. I managed to dodge the club and pick up a stone, which I threw at one of them. He fell down and was knocked out. The other ran away with the pig. Two more came out of the woods, so I decided to run myself. I had no choice but to tell Adam Taydem, the foreman at Ford's lumber mill, since the pig was missing. He rode off to the Indian village, and, with a band of Indians, started out after the robbers. The Indians were good at tracking people in the woods, and they were paid for it. The slaves were all captured, after living as runaways for about three weeks. Taydem got a big reward from the owners.

It was not unusual for a slave to die in trying to run away. There was a slave driver named Augustus on Carey's plantation, next to Epps's. Carey was a rich man with 153 field hands and about that many slave children besides. One day, Augustus ran away and hid in a sugarcane bin, near the top. The dogs found him easily enough, but they couldn't get up to him. So he stayed there, surrounded, until the overseers came and pulled him down. But before the dogs could be pulled away, they had him on the ground and were tearing him to bits. He died the next day.

The most wonderful escape I ever heard of was by one of Carey's girls. She was nineteen or twenty years old, whiter than Carey himself, and her name was Celeste.

I was in my cabin one night, playing my violin just before going to bed, when she burst in. I would have taken her for a ghost, if I were more superstitious. I was surprised and frightened, and thought that she must be some young mistress, quite crazy. But she wore a slave's cotton dress.

"Who are you?" I demanded.

"I'm hungry. Give me some bacon," she said. "My name is Celeste," she told me after I gave her some bacon. "I belong to Carey, and have been in the swamp for two days. I'm sick, and can't work, and would rather die in the swamp than be whipped by the overseer. Carey's dogs won't follow me. There's a secret between them and Celeste, and they won't follow me. Give me some more meat—I'm starving."

Celeste was one of those rare people that the dogs will never follow. No one knows how to explain it. They just won't.

She came to my cabin for food a few nights, but one evening, the dogs barked, and Epps came out to see what was going on. After that I carried food to her at a special place. She lived that way for most of the summer, and got well. But she finally gave herself up. She was whipped and sent back to work in the fields.

The year before I came to the bayou, a whole group of slaves had tried to escape together. It was still the most interesting thing to talk about up and down the bayou years later.

A slave named Lew Cheney decided that the only way to escape was to gather enough men, women, and children, horses, mules, and weapons together, so that they could fight their way across the border into Mexico. A lonely spot in the woods was chosen as their meeting place, and, after a while, a large group of slaves was gathered there, and ready to go. But before they could leave, they were spotted. Lew Cheney, the traitor, decided to save his own life at the expense of everyone else's. He ran to town and told everyone there that the slaves, instead of trying to escape, wanted to kill every white person on the bayou.

You can imagine the panic! The whole band of slaves was rounded up and taken to Alexandria in chains, and hanged there. Many others who were suspected of being anti-white were lynched. The slave-owning planters finally decided to fight against this destruction of their property. But the lynchings didn't stop until a troop of soldiers from the Texas frontier marched into town and tore down the gallows.

Cheney became a hero, and a special act of the state legislature gave him his freedom. Hundreds died, but Cheney, at least, was free.

The idea of rebelling against the planters was not new. More than once we talked about it seriously. But without guns, we had no chance.

I remember our hopes during the Mexican War in 1846 and 1847. American victories were good news in the great houses of the planters, but we slaves would have been glad to see a conquering army of Mexicans.

Wiley suffered badly at the hands of Epps, but not worse than most of the other slaves. He was often enough angry with me.

One day a Mr. O'Neil, a leather tanner, came to

the plantation to talk to Epps about buying me. Aunt Phebe heard them talking and came running to tell me. "Master Epps is going to sell you to a tanner over in the Pine Woods," she said, so loudly that Mrs. Epps could hear what she said.

"Well, Aunt Phebe," I said, "I'm glad of it. I'm tired of picking cotton, and would rather be a tanner. I hope he'll buy me."

But Epps and O'Neil couldn't agree on a price, and the sale was off. A few minutes after O'Neil left, Epps came out with his whip in his hand. Nothing makes a master angrier than hearing that one of his slaves is not perfectly happy, or that he would like to change masters.

"So, Platt," he said to me. "You're tired of picking cotton, are you? You'd like to change masters, eh? You're fond of traveling around—a traveler, eh? Ah, yes—like to travel for your health, maybe? Feel too good for cotton-picking, I suppose. So you're going into the tanning business? Good business—devilish fine business. I think I'll go into that business myself. Down on your knees—I'll try my hand at tanning."

I begged him for mercy, but it was hopeless.

"How do you like your *tanning?*" he asked as he hit me for the first time. "How do you like *tanning?*" he asked at every blow. After about thirty lashes, he let me get up, and promised that if I still liked the business, he would give me more lessons later.

Uncle Abram, too, was often treated badly. One day, Epps came home drunk from Marshall's. He began to give orders, one after the other, each one opposite to the one before. Whatever we did, nothing was right. When Uncle Abram, who was getting old and feeble, made some small mistake, Epps came at him with a knife. He stabbed the old man in the back, a long ugly wound that bled a lot. But Uncle Abram was lucky because it did not go very deep. Mrs. Epps sewed it up and scolded her husband for being so cruel. She warned him that he would make the whole family poor if he went around stabbing slaves.

Every once in a while, Epps would knock Aunt Phebe down with a stick or a chair, but he kept the worst treatment of all for poor Patsey.

Between Epps and Mrs. Epps, she always got the worst of it, but somehow she stayed happy and joyful. One day it was Epps who got jealous, and that was very bad for Patsey.

She had left the plantation for a few hours, while the rest of us were washing our clothes on the bayou bank. Epps looked all over for her, and finally saw her coming over from Shaw's house. Shaw's slave wife, Harriet, knew the trouble Patsey had, and they were friends and visited sometimes.

But Epps could only think of one thing that day —that Patsey was over seeing Shaw himself. He flew into a rage and demanded to know why she was over at Shaw's.

"Missus didn't give me soap to wash with, as she does the rest, and you know why. I went over to Harriet's to get a piece," and she pulled out a bar of soap from her pocket to show him.

"You lie, you black wench," Epps shouted.

"I don't lie, master. Even if you kill me, I'll stick to that story."

"Oh, I'll fetch you down. I'll teach you to go to Shaw's. I'll take the starch out of you." And he ordered me to bring a whip and four stakes.

The stakes were driven into the ground, and poor Patsey was stripped naked. Her arms and legs were tied to the stakes, and I was ordered to whip her. Mrs. Epps and the children watched from the porch. She looked very satisfied.

I hit her a few times.

"Strike harder, or your turn will be next, you scoundrel," Epps yelled.

"Oh, mercy, master, have mercy. Oh God, pity me," Patsey yelled.

I struck her about thirty times and then stopped, hoping that would be enough for Epps. But he ordered me to continue. By this time Patsey's back was covered with long, red welts. Epps was still like a crazy man, wanting to know if she still felt like going to Shaw's, and swearing that he would whip her until she wished she was in hell.

Finally, I threw down the whip and wouldn't whip her any more. Epps grabbed it himself, and whipped her ten times as hard as I had. The lash was wet with blood, which ran down Patsey's sides and onto the ground. After a while, she stopped struggling, and her head sank to the ground. She didn't even scream when the lash bit out small pieces of her flesh. I thought she was dying.

Finally, Epps got too tired to whip her any more.

He ordered Aunt Phebe to wash her down with salt and water and dress her, and I took her back to her cabin. Her dress was soaked through with blood by now, and it was getting stiff as it dried.

Day after day, Patsey lay on the floor of her cabin, face down because her back hurt. She got better after a while, but she was never the same Patsey. Now she was as likely to cry as to laugh. If ever there was a broken heart, it was Patsey's.

Slave owners were wrong when they thought that slaves had no idea of what freedom means. The slaves understand it well enough—they can compare themselves with the white men and see the difference between working for someone else and working for yourself. Patsey's life, especially after the beating, was one long dream of freedom. She had heard that in the North there were no slaves and no masters. And in her mind, it was a magic land—the heaven of the earth.

CHAPTER 11

The Road to Freedom

IN JUNE, 1852, a Mr. Avery, a carpenter who lived near the Bayou Rouge, began building a house for Master Epps. Since I was an experienced carpenter, I was taken out of the fields and put to work with Avery and his assistants. One of them was named Bass, and he was a Canadian, about forty or fifty years old, who had no family alive and no place he called home. For a few years, he had been living in Marksville.

He was very cool and sure of himself. He liked to argue, but he always spoke in the kind of voice that you couldn't get mad at, no matter what he said. Everybody said that he would take the unpopular side of any argument, and no one on the Red River would agree with him on religion or politics. But instead of being angry with him, people found him funny.

He had lived in Illinois before he came to Marksville, and I don't have any idea where he is now. He got his things together and left the day before I did.

One day, while working on the house, Epps and Bass got into a long talk about slavery. I listened carefully.

"I tell you what it is, Epps," Bass said. "It's all wrong, sir. There's no justice nor righteousness in it. I wouldn't own a slave if I was a rich man, which I am not, and that's well understood by all the people I owe money to. That's another thing, the credit system. Credit leads a man into temptation. Cash down is the only thing that will save him. But back to slavery; what right do you have to your slaves, when you come right down to it?"

"What right?" Epps demanded. "Why, I bought them and paid for them!"

"Of course you did. The law says you have the right to hold a slave. But, begging the law's pardon, it lies. Yes, the law is a liar when it says that. Is everything right because the law allows it? Suppose they passed a law taking away your liberty and making you a slave?"

"Oh, that isn't supposable," Epps laughed. "I hope you're not comparing me to a nigger."

"Well," Bass answered, "no, not exactly. But I have seen niggers as good as I am, and I haven't seen any white man in this area that I consider better than myself. Now, what is the difference between a white man and a black one?"

"All the difference in the world," Epps answered, still laughing. "You might as well ask what the difference is between a white man and a baboon. Now, I've seen one of those animals in New Orleans that knew just as much as any nigger I've got. You'd call *them* fellow citizens, I suppose?" He enjoyed his joke.

"Look here, Epps," Bass continued. "You can't laugh me down like that. Some men are witty, and some aren't as witty as they think. Now, let me ask you a question. Are all men created free and equal, as the Declaration of Independence says?"

"Yes. But all men—niggers and monkeys aren't," Epps answered, and laughed even louder than before.

"There are monkeys among white people as well as black. I know some white men who use arguments no monkey would use. But let that pass," Bass said. "These niggers are human beings. If they don't know as much as their masters, whose fault is that? They are not allowed to know anything. You'd whip one of them if you caught him reading a book. If they are baboons, you and men like you have to answer for it. There's a sin resting on this nation that will not go unpunished forever."

"If you lived up among the Yankees in New England," Epps said, "I suppose you'd be one of those fanatics that know more than the Constitution and go around peddling clocks and tempting slaves to run away."

"If I were in New England, I would be just what I am here. I would say that slavery is wrong and ought to be abolished. You have no more right to your freedom than old Uncle Abram over there. Talk about black skin and black blood; how many slaves are there on the bayou who are as white as either of us? The whole system is as absurd as it is cruel. You may own niggers and be damned, but I wouldn't own one for the best plantation in Louisiana."

"You sure like to hear yourself talk, Bass, more than anyone else I know. You would argue that black is white or white is black, if anybody would argue with you over it."

Bass stayed at Epps's for the rest of the summer, and they had conversations like that over and over again. I became sure that Bass was a man I could trust. But I had to be careful; it was not my place to speak to a white man except when spoken to.

It was August and we were alone one afternoon when I decided to do it. I stopped work suddenly and said:

"Master Bass, what part of the country do you come from?"

"Why, Platt, what put that in your head?" he asked, surprised. "You wouldn't know if I told you. I was born in Canada; now guess where that is."

"Oh, I know where Canada is," I said. "I've been there myself."

"Yes, I expect you know that country well," he said, laughing and not believing me.

"As sure as I live, master," I replied, "I've been there. I've been in Montreal and Kingston and Queenston and a lot of places in Canada and in New York State, too—in Buffalo and Rochester and Albany, and I can tell you all the names of the villages along the Champlain Canal."

Bass turned around and stared at me for a long time without saying a word.

"How did you come here?" he asked after a long while.

"Master Bass, if justice were done, I never would have been here at all."

"Who are you? You've been in Canada, sure enough. I know all the places you named. Tell me all about it—how did you get here?"

"I have no friends here I can trust," I said. "I'm afraid to tell you, but I don't think you would tell Master Epps if I did."

He promised me that he would never tell, and, although I'd heard that before from Armsby, I trusted Bass. It was a long story, I told him, and would take time. Master Epps would be back soon, I said, but I'd tell him that night after everyone was asleep.

I came to his cabin late at night and told him my story. He was very interested. I begged him to write to friends of mine in the North, and ask them to free me or send me free papers. Bass agreed, but warned that there was danger in being caught.

So I gave him the names of William Perry, Cephas Parker and Judge Marvin, all of Saratoga Springs. I had worked for the judge at the United States Hotel there, and I had had business with the other two for years. I hoped that at least one of them would still be living there.

This is the letter he wrote for me and mailed from Marksville that Saturday night. One copy went to each of my three friends.

Bayou Boeuf, August 15, 1852

Gentlemen—

It having been a long time since I have seen or heard from you, and not knowing that you are living, it is with uncertainty that I write to you, but the necessity of the case must be my excuse.

Having been born free, just across the river from you, I am certain that you must know me, and I am now a slave. I wish you to obtain free papers for me, and forward them to me at Marksville, Parish of Avoyelles, and oblige,

yours,

Solomon Northup

P.S.—The way I came to be a slave, I was taken sick in Washington City and was insensible for some time. When I recovered my reason, I was robbed of my free papers and in irons on my way to this state; and have never been able to get any-one to write for me until now; and he that is writing for me runs the risk of his life if detected.

We spoke for a few hours after Bass finished writing. He talked about himself in a sad way, as a lonely man, a wanderer about the world. He said that he was growing old, and must soon die, without any relatives or children, and that his life was not worth much to him. He swore that he would use it for getting me back my freedom, and for ending slavery, any way he could.

After that, he did not talk so much about slavery

to Epps, and Epps could not guess that Bass and I knew each other any better than most slaves and white men in the bayous.

Bass figured that it would take the letter two weeks to get there, and two more weeks for an answer to return. Within six weeks, at the most, we told each other, an answer would come, if it was coming at all. At the end of four weeks he went to Marksville again, but there was no letter at the post office. Six, seven, eight, and ten weeks passed, and nothing came. Finally Epps's house was finished, and Bass had to leave. I was frantic—he was my only hope. But he said that he would be back around Christmas, and if no answer had come by then, well, he would see what he could do then.

I did not work well all those months, and often looked sick. No letter came from New York. Finally, around Christmas, Bass came back.

"How are you?" Epps asked, shaking his hand. "Glad to see you."

He would not have been so glad if he knew why Bass had come back.

I stood on the porch of my cabin until after midnight, waiting for Bass to come and talk to me, but he was afraid he might wake up Epps, and so he didn't come. I woke up Uncle Abram one hour earlier than usual in the morning, and sent him into the house to light the fire, which was his chore at this time of year. I gave Bob a shove, and asked him if he intended to sleep until noon. He jumped up frightened, knowing what happened to slaves who overslept, and ran out of the cabin. I was alone, and then after a while, Bass came in.

"No letter yet, Platt," he said.

"Oh, please write again, Master Bass," I begged, heartbroken.

"No use," he answered. "No use. I have made up my mind to that. I'm afraid the postmaster at Marksville is suspicious already—I've been there asking for a letter too often. It's too uncertain, too dangerous.

"Then it's all over," I said. "Oh, God, how can I live the rest of my life here?"

"You're not going to," Bass said, smiling, "unless you die very soon. I've thought this through, and have decided. There are more ways than one to do this, and there is a better and surer way than writing letters. I have a job or two to do, and when I finish in April, I'll have a considerable amount of money. I'm going to Saratoga myself.

"I've lived here long enough, and I might as well live somewhere else. I'm as tired of slavery as you are. If I can succeed in freeing you, it will be a good thing I'll remember all my life. Cheer up. I'm with you, life or death. Goodbye, and God bless you."

I had spent months sad and worried, sure that my friends in Saratoga were dead or, worse, didn't care about me. Now I was happy again, because Bass was going to go north for me and do his best.

But back in Saratoga a lot of things were happening that I had no way of knowing.

Bass's letter to Cephas Parker and William Perry

arrived in Saratoga in early September. My wife, Anne, had moved to Glens Falls, in Warren County, some time before, and she was in charge of the kitchen in Carpenter's Hotel there. She kept house, and cared for our children.

Parker and Perry sent the letter to Anne as soon as they got it. She and the children, who all thought I might have died since that first letter twelve years ago that the English sailor had mailed, were all excited to hear from me. Anne took it to Sandy Hill, to Henry B. Northup, a lawyer whose parents had owned and then freed my father many years ago.

Mr. Northup found a law, passed in 1840, which outlined the way to free a New Yorker kidnapped into slavery in another state. It's called "An act more effectually to protect the free citizens of this state from being kidnapped or reduced to slavery." The law says that the governor, after being given evidence that a citizen is being held in slavery, should name an agent and send him after the New Yorker.

So Mr. Northup took my letter, and the earlier one, to Governor Washington Hunt, who appointed Northup his agent to bring me back. But Northup was running for Congress that year, and he could not come after me until after the election that November. He lost.

But while politics slowed things down, it also speeded things up. Governor Hunt and Mr. Northup both belonged to the same political party, the Whigs. Since they were both Whigs, and both politicians, it was easy for Northup to get an appointment to see the governor. If Bass had written a few months later, things would have been different. Northup, a Whig, would never have gotten to see the new governor, Horatio Seymour, a Democrat.

Well, after he lost the election and rested from the campaign, Northup set out for Washington, D.C. He showed his letters and legal papers from Governor Hunt to Pierre Soule, the senator from Louisiana, and other officials, who all gave him more letters and documents to help him. Senator Soule was especially interested. He said it was the duty of every planter in his state to help free kidnapped slaves, like me, to protect the good name of slavery. Whatever his reasons, he was helpful.

So, on January 1, 1853, Henry Northup got off a steamer at the Marksville landing and went to the courthouse there. He took all his letters and documents to John P. Waddill, a lawyer, and Mr. Waddill promised to help him find and free me. Whatever they thought of slavery, most people there hated kidnappers.

Solomon Northup was a name Mr. Waddill had never heard, but he was sure that if there was a slave with that name in the county, his slave Tom would know him. But of course, Tom didn't know, because I never used that name since leaving Washington years ago.

Since the letter from Bass was dated at Bayou Boeuf, they decided to look for me there. But the bayou was twenty-three miles away, and thousands of slaves live on its banks for fifty or a hundred miles around. Waddill had no idea what to do, except to stop at every plantation on both sides of the bayou and ask for me. This would have failed, I'm sure, since they could hardly have gone into every field and looked at all the slaves on every plantation. They did not know I was known only as Platt. And if they asked Epps himself, or Adam Taydem, or Ford, or anybody, those people would have honestly said that they had never heard of Solomon Northup.

But before going, they decided to wait for Monday morning. They settled down for an afternoon of conversation. The talk turned to New York politics, which the Southerner found very confusing.

Mr. Northup, filling his pipe, began to talk about New York's abolitionists, people who wanted to end slavery. "You have none of those here, do you?" he asked.

"Never, except one," Waddill said, laughing. "We have one here at Marksville, who preaches abolitionism as strongly as any madman in the North. He is a generous, inoffensive man, but always on the wrong side of every argument. He gives us all a lot of fun. He is a carpenter. His name is Bass."

They talked some more about other things, but, after a while, Waddill began to think and stopped talking.

"Let me see—let me s-e-e—" he said, asking to see the letter again. "Bayou Boeuf, August 15, August 15—postmarked here. 'He that is writing for me'— Where did Bass work last summer?" he asked, turning to his younger brother.

"Bass worked last summer somewhere on Bayou Boeuf," he said.

Waddill slammed his fist on the table. "He is the man who can tell us all about Solomon Northup," he yelled.

They finally found Bass, after a long search, just as Bass was getting ready to leave town for a week or two. After being introduced, Northup asked to speak to him privately for a moment.

"Mr. Bass," he said, "can I ask you if you were on Bayou Boeuf last August?"

"Yes, sir, I was there in August," he answered.

"Did you write a letter for a colored man at that place to some gentlemen in Saratoga, New York?"

"That's none of your business," Bass said, staring sharply at Northup for a long time.

"Perhaps I'm being too hasty, Mr. Bass. I beg your pardon. But I have come to do what the letter asks. I think perhaps that you wrote it. I'm looking for Solomon Northup. If you know him, tell me where he is, and I'll never tell who told me."

Bass stared at Northup, trying to decide. He seemed to be doubting whether to trust him or not.

Finally he said with a lot of emotion: "I have done nothing to be ashamed of. I am the man who wrote the letter. If you have come to rescue Solomon Northup, I am glad to see you."

"When did you see him last, and where is he?"

"I saw him at Christmas, a week ago today. He is the slave of Edwin Epps, a planter on Bayou Boeuf, near Holmesville. He is called Platt."

Northup and Waddill went back to Marksville for the evening, intending to set out for the bayou in the morning. But rumors began to float around the town that a New Yorker had come after one of Epps's slaves. So, hoping to get to Epps's before the rumor did, they woke up the sheriff and the judge, and had the necessary documents signed and sealed. Northup and the sheriff set out in the night after me.

The sheriff insisted that they test me about my wife, children, friends in New York, where I was born, etc., because Epps would probably take the whole thing to court, and they wanted proof. The kind of questions only the real Solomon Northup could answer.

Monday morning, January 3, 1853, all the slaves were out in the field very early. It was a raw, cold morning, unusual in that part of the country. I was in the lead row, Uncle Abram was next to me, Bob, Patsey, and Wiley were behind with their cotton bags around their necks. Epps happened to come out that morning without his whip. He swore that we were doing nothing, but it was hard to work in the cold. Epps cursed himself for not bringing his whip, and swore that he would warm us up when he came out again. He would make us hotter than hell, he said.

He left, and we talked among ourselves while picking. But, as we were talking, we saw a carriage pull up. Two men got out. Now it was very unusual for white men to come right up to us in the fields like that, and we were amazed.

The sheriff walked right up to Bob and asked:

"Where is the boy they call Platt?"

"That's him," Bob said, taking off his hat and pointing.

I wondered what the sheriff could want with me.

"Your name is Platt, is it?" he asked.

"Yes, master."

Pointing toward the other white man, he demanded, "Do you know that man?"

I looked at him and suddenly memories came flooding back, memories of Anne and my children, my father and mother, all my friends from happier days, memories of New York.

"*Henry B. Northup!* Thank God, thank God!" I understood right away what was happening and ran toward him.

"Stop a moment," the sheriff said. "Do you have any other name than Platt?"

"Solomon Northup is my name, master."

"Do you have a family?"

"I had a wife and three children."

"What are your children's names?"

"Elizabeth, Margaret, and Alonzo."

"And your wife's name before her marriage?"

"Anne Hampton."

"Who married you?"

"Timothy Eddy of Fort Edward."

"Where does that gentleman live?" he asked, pointing toward Northup.

"He lives in Sandy Hill, Washington County, New York."

He started to ask me more questions, but I brushed past him and grabbed and hugged Northup. I was so happy that I couldn't speak.

"Sol," he said. "I'm glad to see you."

"Throw down that sack," he said, after we stood looking at each other for a while. "Your cotton-picking days are over. Come with us."

We walked toward the great house, and Northup told me that Anne and the children were all well, but that my mother had died. I began to get weak with excitement, and the sheriff had to hold me up as we walked.

Epps was out front of the house. After he shook hands with the sheriff and met Mr. Northup, they all went into the house. Epps sent me to get firewood.

When I came back, they were sitting around a table. There were papers and documents scattered all over, and Northup was reading one of them to Epps. I took my time lighting the fire, and hung about as long as I could. I was going to leave the room when Epps turned to me and asked:

"Platt, do you know this gentleman?"

"Yes, master," I said, "I have known him as long as I can remember."

"Where does he live?"

"He lives in New York."

"Did you ever live there?"

"Born and bred there."

"You were born free, then. Now, you damned nigger," he said, "why didn't you tell me that when I bought you?"

"Master Epps," I said, in a tone different from that slaves used toward their masters. "Master Epps, you did not take the trouble to ask me. Besides, I told one of my masters, the man that kidnapped me, that I was free, and he beat me almost to death for it."

"It seems there has been a letter written for you by someone. Now, who was it?"

I didn't answer.

"I say, who wrote that letter?"

"Perhaps I wrote it myself."

"You haven't been to the Marksville post office and back before dawn. I know that," Epps said.

He tried to get me to tell for a long time, but gave up. Turning to Northup, he swore that if he had only known an hour before he would have run me into the swamp or some other place where all the sheriffs in the world couldn't have found me.

I walked out into the yard, where Aunt Phebe came running up to me. "Lord Almighty, Platt, what do you think? Those two men came after you. I heard them tell the master that you are free, and have a wife and three children back where you came from. Going with them? You're a fool if you don't—I wish I could go."

After a while, Mrs. Epps came out and wondered why I had never told her. She said she was sorry to lose me, that she would rather have lost any other servant on the plantation. Now there was no one who could mend a chair or fix the furniture, no one to play the violin. She began to cry.

The slaves were so interested by all this that they

came out of the field and stood around the yard. Normally that would have earned them all a hundred lashes each.

Epps arranged with Northup and the sheriff to meet the next day in Marksville before the judge, to finish off the legal work of freeing me. Then we walked toward the carriage.

Mrs. Epps came up, and I took off my hat to her.

"Goodbye, missus."

"Goodbye, Platt," she said.

"Goodbye, master," I said to Epps.

"Ah, you damned nigger," he said and spat on the ground.

Patsey ran up to the carriage and threw her arms around me. "You're going away where I'll never see you anymore. You're going to be free. You've saved me a good many whippings, Platt. I'm glad you're going to be free—but what will become of poor Patsey?"

I pulled myself away from her and got in the carriage. The driver cracked his whip, and we were off. I looked back and saw Patsey standing there, her head drooping. Mrs. Epps stood on the porch, Uncle Abram and Bob and Wiley and Aunt Phebe stood by the gate, looking after me. I waved at them, and the carriage turned a bend in the road, and they passed out of sight.

CHAPTER 12

Home Again After Twelve Years

WE STAYED IN New Orleans for two days before heading north to Washington. I saw Theophilus Freeman on the street in New Orleans, but, of course, I didn't say hello. From other people we found out that he had become a broken-down, bad man and lost his business.

We arrived in Washington nine days later, and found that both Birch and Radburn were still living in the city. We went right to the police and swore out a complaint against James H. Birch for kidnapping and selling me into slavery. He was arrested and held in $3,000 bail. He was very excited and afraid when he was first arrested. Before reaching the jail or even knowing exactly what he was being arrested for, he begged the policemen to let him speak to his friend, Benjamin O. Shekell, a slave trader for seventeen

years and his former partner. Shekell later paid his
bail for him.

There was a hearing the next day, January 18,
1853. Henry Northup acted as my lawyer, and Birch
hired a lawyer named Joseph H. Bradley.

Ebenezer Radburn was sworn in as my first witness.
He said that he was forty-eight years old; that he lived
in Washington and had known Birch for fourteen
years; that in 1841 he was the keeper of Birch's slave
pen; and that he remembered keeping me locked up
in the pen that year. At this point, Bradley admitted
that I was in the pen that year. Radburn was our only
witness, and we rested our case.

Then Bradley called Benjamin Shekell. He said
that he was the owner of the Steamboat Hotel in
Washington in 1841, and saw me there in the spring
of that year. He said that two white men came to his
hotel and said that they had a black man for sale.
He remembered that they met Birch and told him
that the black man was a bricklayer and played the
violin. Shekell said I was the black man they were
talking about. He said I told Birch that I was born
and bred in Georgia, and that I was very unhappy to
leave my young master, and that I almost cried. I
insisted, Shekell told the judge, that my master had
the right to sell me because my master "had been
gambling and on a spree."

I saw right there that I was going to hear a lot of
lying before we were through.

He said that Birch questioned me and told me that
if he bought me, he would send me south. I said I

had nothing against that, he testified. He said Birch paid $650 for me, and gave me another name, not Solomon, but one he couldn't remember. He said that I and the two white men, whose names he also didn't remember, were in his hotel for about two or three hours, and that I played the violin for them. He said he was Birch's partner before 1838, and their business was buying and selling slaves. After that, Birch was the partner of Theophilus Freeman of New Orleans.

Then a man named Benjamin A. Thorn testified that he was at Shekell's in 1841 and saw a black man playing the violin. "Shekell said he was for sale," Thorn said. "I heard his master tell him he should sell him. The boy told me he was a slave. I was there when the money was paid. I can't say positively that this is the boy. The master came near tears. I think the boy cried."

He said he was a slave trader on and off for twenty years. "When I can't do that, I do something else," he said.

I was then offered as a witness, but the court decided that I couldn't testify. Since it was already proven that I was a free New Yorker and not a slave, the only reason they wouldn't let me testify was because I am black.

Shekell testified that there was a bill of sale signed at the time of the sale, and the judge asked Birch to show it. But Birch swore that, while he had signed a bill of sale, *he had lost it!* The judge didn't quite believe that and sent a policeman to Birch's office to bring back his records book. The policeman brought it back, but there was no record of my purchase or sale in it.

After thinking over the evidence, the judge decided that Birch came by me honestly and innocently, and let him go.

As if that wasn't bad enough, Birch and his friends had me arrested for conspiracy with two white men to cheat him out of $650 by selling myself to him. I had been ready for a little lying, but not this.

Northup acted as my lawyer again. But before the trial could begin, Birch's lawyer persuaded him to drop the ridiculous charge, and I was let go.

We left Washington in disgust January 20, and I gave up any hope of ever getting justice. I wanted nothing more to do with judges and courts and policemen and lying witnesses.

We arrived in Sandy Hill on the evening of January 21, and the next morning I started out for Glens Falls, where Anne and our children now lived.

Margaret was the first one to see me as I entered their cottage. She did not recognize me. When I left her, she was just a little girl, seven years old. Now she was a grown woman. She was married and had a little boy of her own. But she had not forgotten me—she had named the boy Solomon. Anne came running in from the hotel, and then Alonzo and Elizabeth, and you can imagine the joy and crying and hugging that went on. It had been twelve years since we were all together.

A few weeks later, a lawyer named David Wilson,

who had just been elected to the State Assembly, arranged to help me sell my story and get it published. I got $3,000 for it, and bought a piece of land next to Margaret's with the money. I lived with Anne and Alonzo and Elizabeth and became a carpenter.

The book of my adventures as a slave was a success. At first, 8,000 copies were printed, and they were all sold the first month. In the next few years, more than 30,000 more were sold. Many copies were bought by people living in the Red River country of Louisiana.

One of those 38,000 copies was read by a man named Thaddeus St. John, a county judge in Fonda, New York, a small town not far from Saratoga Springs. He read the book, and the more he read, and the more he thought about it, the more he began to remember something that had happened to him years before.

In 1841 he took a trip to Washington, and, while spending the night in Baltimore on the way, he met two old friends, Alexander Merrill and Joseph Russell, who were traveling with a black man.

His friends were acting very strange, Judge St. John recalled. He came up to Russell, surprised to see him, and shouted, "What are you doing here, Joe?" Merrill rushed over to him and urged him not to use their real names.

Later, he met the same three men again in Washington, just before William Henry Harrison's funeral. He left them drinking in a hotel barroom at about 8 P.M. and didn't see them again until he arrived in Baltimore on the way back to New York.

This time, the two white men were alone, and they looked a lot richer. Their long hair was cut, their beards were shaven, their clothes were new, and they had ivory canes and gold watches. Surprised by their new wealth, the judge suggested laughingly that they must have sold their friend for $500. Merrill laughed and told him to add on $150. When the judge questioned him more about it, however, he said that they won it gambling with Southerners.

Well, the judge went home and forgot all about it until he read my book. One day, I got a letter asking to meet him in Fonda, but not explaining why. We recognized each other right away. I was the man he had seen with his two friends.

While I was sick of the law and lawyers and courts, I still wanted justice, so I went to Henry Northup and told him the news.

After asking around for a few months, we found Merrill at his parents' home at the village of Wood Hollow, and had him arrested. He was a dangerous man, and when Northup and the sheriff and I burst into his room, he was sleeping with a knife and a pair of guns by his side.

The police picked up Russell two days later. He was working as a boat captain on the Erie Canal. The two men were brought to Ballston Spa, the county seat, not far from Saratoga Springs, for a hearing. Both Judge St. John and I told our stories in court on July 14, 1854.

The defense lawyers could only argue that New York law didn't allow a trial more than three years after a crime was committed. Mr. Northup solved that problem by arguing that the crime was committed over and over again every minute that I was held as a slave. The court agreed and held them in $5,000 bail for a trial in the fall.

The trial opened in Ballston Spa on October 4, 1854, before a large crowd. But the defense lawyer got it put off until statements could be gotten from Birch and Shekell in Washington.

The trial was continued in February, and letters from Birch and Shekell were shown to the judge. Birch told the same lies all over again, and even made up more.

"I told him," Birch wrote, "that if I bought him, I should send him south. He replied that he would rather go south, as he was raised in a southern country. I asked him who he knew in Georgia, and he mentioned a few names which I don't remember now. In order to make sure that everything was all right, I told him that if I bought him, I would send him to the cotton fields, where he would be badly beaten, and that I intended to whip him as a sample of what he would get. He answered: 'My master has a right to sell me, and I must submit.' I will further state that after the sale of the Negro to me by Brown, both appeared to be very much affected, and both cried."

Shekell sent a letter saying just about the same thing. The defense lawyers, however, realized that while that sort of thing might do in Washington, no court in New York would believe it. So they didn't even introduce the letters as evidence, but based their defense on legal technicalities.

The charges brought against the kidnappers were based on two laws. One made it illegal to kidnap or coax a Negro out of the state in order to sell him into slavery. The other made it a crime to sell a Negro into slavery.

The two men pleaded not guilty to the first charge, and argued that, since the sale took place in Washington, New York courts had no right to try them for it. Since the first offense carried only a ten-year jail sentence, Northup refused to let it go at that.

A court battle went on for years, from court to court, over whether New York courts could try them for selling me in Washington. After a while, the newspapers, which had reported the case on page one every day, lost interest and didn't even cover it.

The case was dropped years later, after everyone, even I, no longer cared about it. I never did get justice, but being free and being home was all I really wanted, anyway.

SOLOMON NORTHUP never won justice. All he did get for the dozen years stolen from his life was the $3,000 he was paid for his book. He bought land in Glens Falls with it and lived there with his family. Northup went back to being a carpenter. After that, nothing more is known about him. But it is known that his wife and son-in-law sold the property and moved away in 1863. Solomon Northup must have died that year, at the age of fifty-five. It was the tenth year of his regained freedom, the third year of the Civil War. It was also the year of the Emancipation Proclamation.

MICHAEL KNIGHT, who has adapted Solomon Northup's story, is a reporter for *The New York Times*.